A crash course
Pascal

Donald M Monro
Imperial College of Science and Technology
University of London

Edward Arnold

First published 1985
by Edward Arnold (Publishers) Ltd
41 Bedford Square, London WC1B 3DQ

ISBN 0 7131 3553 0

To Duncan

There is plenty of time to win this game,
and to thrash the *****ards too.
>   *Sir Francis Drake*

Printed in Great Britain by
Thomson Litho Ltd, East Kilbride, Scotland

Preface

I dedicate this crash course in Pascal to my nephew Duncan Monro who is a real person.

Prompted by evangelical computer scientists who are often better at theorem proving than computer programming anyway, the faculties of schools, colleges and universities have widely adopted the elegant Pascal as a teaching language, which is no bad thing. But at the same time mystification and formalism have followed it into the classroom. The level of distress introduced there among real people has brought anguished cries for the re-introduction of trial by immersion for the perpetrators of this unnecessary cruelty.

I have often been faced by students bitterly disappointed with their grades who claim that a program which works must be good. That is nonsense, as is readily illustrated. However the over-reaction among teachers to this student attitude has been to assert that a program is good if it is beautiful, whether it works or not. That is even greater nonsense in my opinion.

Real people need to write programs. They have real reasons for wanting to do so. It is for real people that I have attempted a practical, de-mystified approach to programming in Pascal. I hope they will learn to write programs which work well and are fairly well structured. Effective ones, in other words. It would be enough for me to please a few real people in this manner. But it would be a real bonus if I can irritate a few formalists along the way.

When you finish your book, you write your Preface in which you say what you feel about it all. I feel exhausted. I will probably not write anything else for at least a week. An outstanding feature of the development process is that Jan Williams and I have been able to work with an improved interactive typesetter by Monro (me) and Murphy (James). Thank you both (Jan and James) for your tireless efforts, and also Jane Spurr for penning some diagrams. Those who really suffer are the members of one's family and I apologise again, but they have heard it all before. Now, I wonder, how about that book on graphics that I have always wanted to write? Or perhaps our efforts on the typesetter qualify us uniquely to undertake the definitive study of underwater text processing. Or maybe . . .

D M Monro
London
April 1985

Contents

One

Introduction

1 About Pascal

Blaise Pascal was a person; a mathematical and scientific all-rounder who lived from 1632 to 1662. When he was 19 (towards the middle of his productive life!) he invented a mechanical calculator which was produced commercially, and some survive today. It was not quite the first calculator, but then Schikart would not make such a nice name for a computing language.

Pascal the computer language was designed by Professor Niklaus Wirth of the ETH, Zurich, for teaching, and was intended to express basic concepts of computing clearly and naturally. That, of course, was itself a comment on the suitability of previous languages for illustrating the principles of programming. Pascal has been taken up by the computing community in a much wider context than this, and has become a seriously used language as well as a teaching vehicle.

Why has it grown so quickly? Mainly because in Pascal clear and well-structured programs flow readily from the hands of experienced programmers. The language is not large and so it is easily implemented on computers of widely varying size. The language has spread in more or less its original form and therefore the 'portability' of programs is excellent. The language has been standardized early in its life, and so the core of the language—ISO Pascal—should remain stable.

2 Formal or informal

Perhaps because of its origins in computer science, many descriptions of Pascal tend to be rather formal. It is harder to describe a computer language correctly in plain words than in the dreaded Extended Backus-Naur Notation, but it is more helpful to real people. Because Pascal has spread so widely, those who need formal descriptions are now greatly outnumbered by these real people to whom I direct my course. The ISO standard itself, freely available from every national standards institution, would satisfy anyone's thirst for formality in a completely authoritative manner. I will try to describe Pascal clearly in plain language.

Blaise Pascal himself wrote, 'I have made this letter longer than usual because I lacked the time to make it short.' I will take the trouble to be concise, mainly to create room for lots and lots of examples. From time to time I inject a summary of previous items.

3 Theory or practice

Computer programming is a practical subject. You can do it well or badly, but either way you need practice. This book is rich in examples and exercises, many of them short. This is to encourage you to try things out by providing you with models of programming. You must have access to a computer which will run Pascal, and an interactive facility is greatly preferred. This means that you can enter Pascal programs through a keyboard, run them interactively, and edit them, preferably on a screen. It does not matter whether you use your own small computer or a larger machine shared with others. What really matters is that you do as much actual programming as possible. The best way to answer a 'What if...?' question about Pascal is to try it.

4 About subsets

This course begins by emphasizing the procedural part of the Pascal language—how you do things rather than the objects that you do them to. By studying from the beginning, you are covering an increasingly full subset of Pascal and by the end you have done it all. However, it is deliberately organized to allow you to stop at any point with a subset of standard ISO Pascal which should work on any computer. Where a facility depends on the machine, I will tell you so. The ISO standard itself describes two levels of Pascal. This will not matter to you except when using 'arrays' in Chapters 12 to 14. There I will point out to you the differences.

I have chosen to introduce Pascal in this unusual order to allow either a quick conversion from another language or a quick introduction for the novice. I have deliberately left the powerful data structuring facilities to the end in the belief that they are of interest mainly to those who make computer programming the central issue in their careers, rather than an incidental one. That is not to say that this is an incidental course. It is a perfectly serious introduction to Pascal, with the emphasis on data structures adjusted to suit real people.

5 A crash course

I have organized this book to take you rapidly through the essentials of Pascal. Our objective is to learn as quickly as possible to write well-organized, readable and effective programs. As a conversion course it should only take a few days to master the basics, assuming unlimited access to a suitable computer. As an introduction, how long it takes depends on how far and how intensively it is studied. Before you start, arrange for a computer to use and line up your friendly adviser. Then begin at the beginning and take it all in order.

When you come to an exercise, work it out on paper before approaching the computer—it is harder to think at the keyboard and the results are never as good. You should spend at least twice as much time in practice as in study. Do lots of exercises and a selection of problems. Never will so many learn so much in such a short time. Have a nice day!

Two

Simple programs

1 An actual program

This is a computer program written in Pascal:

```
program howdy;
   begin
     writeln('Hi there, Tex')
   end.
```

Although it does not do much, this program contains a number of important elements. The program consists of four lines, each having a clear meaning. Most people write Pascal in this way, with a new item of the program on each line. However, this is not always the case because the layout of a Pascal program is quite flexible. This program would have the same meaning if written

```
program howdy; begin writeln('Hi there, Tex') end.
```

although it is probably not as readable.

The order of items in a Pascal program is more rigid than in many other programming languages. This bit of discipline is one of the things that makes Pascal easy to understand, because items always occur in an expected place.

A program consists of *declarations* and *actions*. The declarations come first and the actions come last. The line

```
program howdy;
```

is a declaration. It says, "This is a program whose name is 'howdy'." Every Pascal program must begin with a **program** declaration. Although it does nothing, it may mean something to your computer.

The three lines

```
   begin
     writeln('Hi there, Tex')
   end.
```

are the action part of the program. The action part always begins with **begin** and ends with **end**. The period after **end** is necessary to indicate the end of the program. **Begin, end** and

program are keywords of Pascal which are shown in bold type in the body of this text, but not in the examples which are inserted unaltered into the text from my computer.

The middle line of the action part

```
writeln('Hi there, Tex')
```

is called a *statement*. Statements are the items of Pascal which actually cause things to happen. This one writes a line on the output device, which is probably a screen or a printer. *Writeln* is the name of a procedure for output. The names of things in Pascal, called *identifier*s, are shown in italics in the body of this text but not in the examples.

The punctuation of the program is also important. Declarations and/or statements are separated by semicolons. A program always ends with the word **end** followed by a period.

> *Exercise* Learn to use Pascal on your computer now. Find out how to enter the four line program, edit it (because everyone's typing is imperfect), and run it. Beginners may have to struggle a bit with the computer system. It is vital to spend an hour or so on this now, while the Pascal is easy.

2 Messages

The actual program

```
program howdy;
  begin
    writeln('Hi there, Tex')
  end.
```

wrote a message 'Hi there, Tex' (especially for railway enthusiasts) on the screen or printer. A message like that is known as a string of characters, or, more precisely, a *string constant*. Any series of symbols known to your computer can be written in quotation marks to make a string constant—but be careful to use single quotes rather than double ones. These are some string constants:

```
'Hi there, Tex'
'track 29'
'2+2'
```

To use a quotation mark inside a string constant, put two of them—otherwise it will be interpreted as the end of the string and the program will be rejected. These are correct:

```
'The bee''s knees'
'To get '' put ''''.'
```

Look carefully at the second one.

The *writeln* procedure writes things on an output device and then begins a new line. Several items can be written, separated by commas:

```
writeln('one','two','three')
```

or a *writeln* can write nothing, except that it will produce a new line:

```
writeln
```

A *write* statement also produces output, but after *write* another *write* or *writeln* continues on the same line. The difference between *write* and *writeln* is exploited by programmers in organizing lines of output. The rule is simple:

A new line comes after *writeln*.

Those converting from another language to Pascal will easily adjust; the decision about a new line is made after *write* or *writeln*, not before.

> *Exercise* Try these examples which will highlight the difference between *write* and *writeln* (and also show how Pascal differs from other languages). Notice that semicolons are used to separate the series of statements which appear between **begin** and **end**.

```
program one;
  begin
    write('This write is followed');
    write(' by this write.')
  end.
```

```
program two;
  begin
    write('This write is followed');
    writeln(' by this writeln');
    writeln('and another writeln too.')
  end.
```

Notice the space before the word 'by'. What happens if it is left out?

```
program three;
  begin
    write('Two writes are separated');
    writeln;
    write('by a writeln.')
  end.
```

```
program four;
  begin
    writeln('Two writelns are separated');
    writeln;
    writeln('by a writeln.')
  end.
```

3 The form of programs—comments

A simple Pascal program consists of a *block*. This block is made up of a *declaration part* and an *action part*:

> *block   declaration part;*
> *action part*

In this chapter, the absolute minimum declaration part has been used, consisting of the compulsory **program** declaration:

```
program name;
```

The minimum action part would have only **begin** and **end**:

```
begin
end.
```

but would be fairly useless. An action part consists of:

> **begin**
> *statement;*
> *statement;*
> .
> .
> *statement*
> **end**.

The period occurs only at the end of a Pascal main program, which in the simple examples of this chapter have exactly one block.

The semicolon in Pascal is used to separate statements and/or declarations from one another. For the time being it is easiest to regard the semicolon as required after a statement or a declaration, except for the last statement before **end**. In Chapter 8, the placing of the semicolon will be clarified.

It is because of the semicolon used to separate items that several statements or declarations of Pascal can be put on one line, as in the program

```
program howdy; begin writeln('Hi there, Tex') end.
```

There is no required relationship between the lines of a program as it is written and its meaning. Declarations and/or statements are separated from each other by semicolons, and other items are separated by one or more spaces, a special symbol, or the occurrence of a new line. Therefore a programmer has great flexibility in the layout of a program. The beginnings of an indentation scheme will be noticed in this chapter. Most good programmers use indentation to make the structures of their programs stand out (or in), and it will be seen that this is very helpful in making a program readable.

Programs can also be made clear by adding helpful comments. In Pascal these can be inserted anywhere at all before the final period except inside a string constant. Normally a comment is placed in curly brackets, like this:

```
{ this is a comment }
```

In the middle of a string constant, this would be part of the string, not a comment. Otherwise a comment will also act as a separator just like a blank or a new line.

```
writeln('None of { this is a comment }.')
```

Some computers do not accept curly brackets, so the symbol pairs (* and *) can also be used to delimit comments:

```
(* This is also a comment *)
{ So is this *)
```

Here is a program with comments added; perhaps too many for such a simple example:

```
{A friendly demonstration program}

{The minimum declaration part comes first}

program friendly;

{The action part is also somewhat brief}

  begin

    {Only one statement here — no semicolon}

    writeln('I like you.')
  end.
```

4 Some items summarized

At the end of this book there is a concise summary of Pascal, which can be referred to for any of the rules and constructions of the language.

Here is a review of the items introduced in this chapter.

(i) A simple program consists of:

declaration part
action part

(ii) The **program** declaration identifies the program:

program *identifier*;

(iii) The action part consists of

> **begin**
>   *statement*;
>   *statement*;
>
>   .
>
>   .
>
>   .
>
>   *statement*
> **end**.

(iv) The period after **end** terminates a program.

(v) The semicolon separates declarations and/or statements from one another.

(vi) The *write* procedure

> *write*(*item, item, ...*)

writes information on an output device. The next *write* or *writeln* will continue writing on the same line.

(vii) The *writeln* statement

> *writeln*(*item, item, ...*)

writes information on an output device and then begins a new line.

(viii) A string constant is any series of symbols enclosed in single quotes. To include a single quote, put two of them.

(ix) A comment is any series of symbols beginning either with { or (* and ending with either } or *), unless these are part of a string constant.

5 Problems

Problem 2.1 Write this on the screen or printer:

```
Be careful not to fall off the

                          end of

                    the pier!

                Splash.
```

Problem 2.2 Write a topical limerick on the screen or printer using a Pascal program with several *writeln* statements. Be careful who is watching before selecting a rude or polite one. Then make it double space with extra *writeln* statements.

Three
Working with real numbers

1 Real arithmetic—constants and expressions

Calculating is a fundamental use of computers. There are two basic kinds of numbers in Pascal (and many other languages) which are *integer* and *real* numbers. An integer takes an exact whole value, like 1 or 2 or 34 or −73.

There are some interesting and subtle effects in using integers which are described in the next chapter. Real numbers are those with decimal places, like 3.1416 or 1.0. Often computers can only give approximate results with real numbers because the number of decimal places is always restricted by the precision of the computer.

There are two forms of real constants. A number can be written with the decimal point in the natural place, as in

$$3.14 \qquad -2.0 \qquad +35769.25$$

or a number can be be scaled by a power of ten as in scientific notation:

3 e+10	means	3.0×10^{10}	or	30000000000
2.1 e−6	means	2.1×10^{-6}	or	.0.0000021

Scientific notation has to be written with the power of ten signed, and only an integer power can be used:

$$number \quad \begin{matrix} e \\ or \\ E \end{matrix} \quad sign\ integer$$

This little program does a real calculation which any computer should do exactly:

```
program addem;
  begin
    write(2.5+3.25)
  end.
```

Note that in the *write* statement an expression is used which involves the real constants 2.5 and 3.25.

In the above program, a sum is done, indicated by the symbol + between two values. Not surprisingly, + stands for addition. To define this more precisely, the + symbol is a *dyadic operator*, meaning that it acts on the two values on either side of it, which are its operands.

(The term *binary* is often used instead of dyadic—both mean 'having two operands'.) There are four dyadic operations in the real arithmetic of Pascal:

+	addition	example	2.1+3.2	is 5.3
—	subtraction	example	3.2 − 2.1	is 1.1
*	multiplication	example	2.1 * 3.2	is 6.72
/	division	example	6.25/2.5	is 2.5

There is no operator for raising a number to a power, and how to do this is discussed later in this chapter.

In forming an expression, the question of its interpretation will often arise. For example, does the expression

1.0+2.0*3.0	mean the same as	(1.0+2.0)*3.0, value 9.0
	or the same as	1.0+(2.0*3.0), value 7.0

With round brackets, the meaning is clarified. Every left bracket has to be balanced by a right bracket, as in 1.0+2.0*(3.0+4.0*(5.0+6.0)). To decide what the expression means without brackets, it is necessary to know in what order arithmetic is done. This is specified by a priority rule for arithmetic which is the same as in most other languages. The priority of operations is:

highest	( )	expressions in brackets
	* /	multiplication and division
lowest	+ —	addition and subtraction

When operations are of equal priority they are done from left to right. Therefore

1.0+2.0*3.0   has the value 7.0

In addition, both + and − have a role as the sign of a value, or stated more precisely, they can be used as monadic (or unary) operators which take one operand, to their right.

−(1.0+2.0)	is −3.0
1.0+ −2.0	is −1.0

Exercise Work out mentally the value of the following expressions. Then try them in Pascal. Aim for a perfect score!

```
8.0+2.0/5.0          4.0/5.0+3.0              4.0/(5.0+3.0)
8.0+2.0/5.0+2.5      (8.0+2.0)/5.0+2.5
8.0+2.0/(5.0+2.5)    (8.0+2.0)/(5.0+2.5)
```

Example Tax is charged on goods at 15%. If you know the cost of goods without tax, then the price with tax can easily be computed. This program adds tax to an item worth $5.00:

```
program addtax;
  begin
    writeln('After tax you pay ',5.00*1.15)
  end.
```

That is easy. You can also take the tax away. If it costs $1.00 with tax, what was it before tax at 15%? No, it was not $0.85. Try this:

```
program removtax;
   begin
      writeln('Before tax it was ',1.00/1.15)
   end.
```

Exercise Write a program to find the average of three values (and test it). Can you write the expression without any brackets?

2 Identifiers in Pascal

In Pascal, as in all computer languages, values are manipulated by giving them names. *Identifiers* (names) in Pascal can be any sequence of letters or numbers as long as the first symbol is a letter. Identifiers cannot include blanks or other special symbols.

These are some correct names, and all of them are different:

i	*name*	*ThisIsLong*
x3j3	*z123*	*SillyMoo*

Upper and lower case letters have the same meaning everywhere in Pascal except in character variables (Chapter 13) and character string constants. Therefore all of these are the same name:

```
this This tHis thIs thiS
THis ThIs ThiS tHIs tHiS
```
and so on.

The ISO standard for Pascal requires that all the letters and numbers should be significant in an identifier. In may versions of Pascal, this rule is violated. Often only the first 8 letters actually identify a name and the rest are ignored. In making programs as transportable as possible, this state of affairs should be borne in mind. These two names may not be the same:

```
TheseMightBeTheSame
TheseMightBeDifferent
```

In Pascal the keywords of the language may not be used as identifiers. This is a list of the reserved words in standard Pascal:

and	**do**	**function**	**nil**	**program**	**type**
array	**downto**	**goto**	**not**	**record**	**until**
begin	**else**	**if**	**of**	**repeat**	**var**
case	**end**	**in**	**or**	**set**	**while**
const	**file**	**label**	**packed**	**then**	**with**
div	**for**	**mod**	**procedure**	**to**	

Any other identifiers can be used by a program for its own purposes. There are, however, a number of additional identifiers which have a meaning because they are the names of facilities provided by Pascal. It is possible, but usually silly, to take them over for some other purpose. A good example of this is *writeln*, the name of a procedure that has already been introduced. Others are *real* (a type), *sqrt* (a function), and *true* (a constant). There are many more.

3 Real variables and assignment

Identifiers are used for several things, and one of these is to name real variables. A real variable is given a name in a **var** declaration:

> **var** *identifier, identifier . . ., identifier: type*;
> *identifier, identifier . . ., identifier: type*;
> .
> .
> .

For example,

```
    var eggs, bacon: real;
```

All variables used by a program must be declared by **var**. The **var** declaration must be placed after the **program** declaration and before the action part. There are other declarations whose order is important, and their proper place is described both when they are introduced and in a summary in Chapter 6. You can also refer to the Appendix.

A variable is undefined when the action part of a Pascal program commences. This means that it has no value, and it is an error to attempt to use its value, for example in an expression or a *writeln* statement. A variable has to be given a value before it can be used. There are only two ways of doing this—in an assignment statement or in a statement which reads the value from a file.

The assignment statement is like this:

> *identifier*:=*value*

The *value* could be the name of a variable whose value is already defined, or a numerical constant, or an expression which calculates a numerical value. When this value is worked out, it is assigned to the variable named on the left hand side. A conversion from integer to real may take place as the assignment is done. We will see in Chapter 4 that an integer can always be substituted for a real anyway (but not the other way around). If you are converting to Pascal from another language, note that two symbols (:=) denote assignment.

> *Example* In the tax programs from a few pages back, variables could be used for the tax rate, the net amount and the gross amount. Note how the choice of names for these variables explains what they are:

```
program add2;
   var netsum,grossum,taxrate:real;
   begin
     taxrate:=Ø.15;
     netsum:=5.Ø;
     grossum:=netsum*(1.Ø+taxrate);
     write('After tax you pay',grossum)
   end.
```

```
program remov2;
   var netsum,grossum,taxrate:real;
   begin
     taxrate:=Ø.15;
     grossum:=1.Ø;
     netsum:=grossum/(1.Ø+taxrate);
     write('Before tax it was',netsum)
   end.
```

4 Repeat forever

A Pascal program controls the order of events in its action part using structured statements. The full range of these will be introduced in Chapters 5 to 8. In the meantime it will be useful to make a series of statements repeat over and over. To do this we use the **repeat** . . . **until** *false* structure:

> **repeat**
> > *statement*;
> > *statement*;
> >
> > .
> >
> > .
> >
> > .
> >
> > *statement*
> **until** *false*

All the statements within the structure will be repeated forever. Note that there need not be a semicolon before the keyword **until**, although Pascal will allow it. Remember that semicolons are used to separate declarations or statements from each other. The keyword **until** is not the beginning of a new statement—it is part of the **repeat** . . . **until** statement. Therefore no semicolon is needed before the word **until**.

> *Exercise* How can a runaway program be stopped in an interactive computer? It is important to know this. Find out (from an expert if necessary) and then run this program:

```
program maverick;
   begin
     repeat
       write('Stop me!  ')
     until false
   end.
```

Pascal can count. See how this program replaces the value of the real variable counter with each repetition:

```
program counts;
  var counter:real;
  begin
    counter:=1.0;
    repeat
      counter:=counter+1.0;
      writeln(counter)
    until false
  end.
```

Example Tax is like compound interest except that it is not usually applied over and over again even though it may sometimes feel like it. The same formula applies:

$$gross = net * (1 + rate)^{periods}$$

This program compounds interest (or tax) forever. Again this is a program which replaces the variable *amount* in each repetition. Repeated replacement of an old value by a new one is called iteration:

```
program compound;
  var amount,rate:real;
  begin
    amount:=1.0;
    rate:=0.15;
    repeat
      writeln('Now we have $',amount);
      amount:=amount*(1.0+rate)
    until false
  end.
```

Exercise In a repeating program:
(i)   Make a counter that increases by five each time.
(ii) Make a value double each time.
(iii) Make a value square each time. If the starting value is greater than one, before long it will be too large for your computer. It would be useful for you to find out the the approximate size of the largest real number on your computer. If the starting value is less than one, it will eventually become too small for your computer to distinguish from zero. It would also be useful to find out small this is.

5 Reading in values

The value of all variables is undefined when the action part begins. A variable can be defined by an assignment statement, as has been seen. The other way to define a variable is to read it from a file. In an interactive system, the usual input file is a keyboard, and the *read* or *readln* procedures are used to request values from it:

read(identifier, identifier . . ., identifier)

When a Pascal program comes to a *read* statement, it looks for correct values from the input file for the variables which are named by the *identifiers*. At a keyboard, these are simply typed in with consecutive values separated by any number of spaces or newlines. (If you are used to other languages, don't use commas.)

> *Exercise* (very important) Here is a program for practising input. Two real variables, *a* and *b*, have their values defined in a *read* statement:

```
program try;
  var a,b:real;
  begin
    repeat
      write('Enter two reals ');
      read(a,b);
      writeln;
      writeln(a,b)
    until false
  end.
```

Use this program to learn how to give real values to a Pascal program. Notice in the program:

(i)   A *write* statement tells the user what is required. Otherwise a person might sit at the keyboard waiting forever for something to happen. In an interactive program always prompt for input in this way.

(ii)   When the input is typed, it appears on the same line as the prompt. Why?

(iii) A *writeln* statement forces a new line before the output is presented by another *writeln*.

Find out what happens if:

(i)   You enter a value including a decimal point.
(ii)   You enter an integer (no decimal point).
(iii) You enter a value in scientific notation with an exponent—don't forget the sign of the exponent.
(iv) You enter a value preceded by a + or − sign.
(v)   You try to enter only one value—push return several times!
(vi) You make a mistake by putting an incorrect symbol in a value.

How can you escape from this program on your computer?

The *readln* statement is the same as *read* except that, after all the values have been obtained, the program proceeds to another new line. On an interactive terminal, this is how to put a prompting message on the same line as the response to it. Try this:

```
program prompter;
  var value:real;
  begin
    repeat
      write('Please enter a real value ..');
      readln(value);
      writeln('Thank you for the ',value:8:3)
    until false
  end.
```

6 Writing out real values

Until now, the output from a *write* or *writeln* procedure has been in scientific notation, except in the most recent example. It is possible (easy, even) for the program to specify a different form of layout. Simply follow a real *item* in the *write* statement by one or two integer expressions, like this:

> *item*:*width*
> *item*:*width*:*decimalplaces*

width and *decimalplaces* are integer values—they could be expressions. Their values must be 1 or greater.

The three possible forms of output are therefore:

> *write*(*item*, . . .)   {or *writeln*}

The output is produced in scientific notation using a number of columns which is always the same on a particular computer, but which varies between computers.

> *write*(*item*:*width*, . . .)   {or *writeln*}

The output is produced in scientific notation and takes up exactly *width* columns. The minimum value of *width* depends on the computer, but must provide for the exponent, the sign of the exponent, some digits, a decimal place and possibly a sign for the digits. The minimum practical value is about 7.

> *write*(*item*:*width*:*decimalplaces*)   {or *writeln*}

The output is displayed in normal notation with the specified number of *decimalplaces* which must be 1 or greater. Clearly *width* must be greater than the number of *decimalplaces* and should allow for the largest value expected. Using this method, errors are possible—it depends on how the computer responds to an impossible combination.

Example An ageing tortoise approaches the elixir of life which is 200 metres away. Today it travels 100 metres, tomorrow 50, and so on with the distance covered reduced to half every day. It is another kind of iteration. This program monitors its progress, showing the total distance covered as a real number, always with three decimal places:

```
program agony;
  {Program evaluates the series
   100 + 50 + 25 + ... }
  var total,today:real;
  begin
    {Set initial values}
    total:=100.0;
    today:=100.0;
    repeat
      {Show progress to date}
      write('Today''s progress is',today:8:3);
      writeln(' making a total of',total:8:3);
      {and do the next iteration}
      today:=today/2.0;
      total:=total+today
    until false
  end.
```

Exercise Discover what happens if you make the following errors:

(i)   An error in the specification *item*:*width* which asks for too small a *width*.

(ii) An error in *item*:*width*:*decimalplaces* in which the number of *decimalplaces* is greater than *width*.

(iii) A program with a correct *item*:*width*:*decimalplaces* specification tries to write too large a number.

7 Give a constant a name

It is useful to be able to give a name to a constant. This may save having to remember a lot of constants, and can make it easier to alter a program if the value of the constant can be changed in only one place. In Pascal the **const** declaration gives a name to a constant. It belongs after the **program** declaration and before the **var** declaration.

> **const** *identifier* = *constant*;
>   *identifier* = *constant*;
>   .
>   .
>   .

A real constant can be a signed number either in scientific notation or with a decimal point. It can also be the name of another real constant with an optional sign. (If an integer number is used, the constant will be of type integer.)

Example This constant declaration defines a number of real constants:

```
const pie = 3.14159265;
      minuspie = -pie;
      avogadro = 6.025e23;
      planck = 6.625e-27;
```

The ISO standard for Pascal requires every name to be defined before it can be used to do anything. This includes defining another name in the same declaration. Fortunately, the definition takes effect immediately. The only exception to the '*define it before you use it*' rule applies to the pointer type introduced in Chapter 18:

```
{You can do this}          {This is wrong}
const top = 5;             const bot = -top;
      bot = -top;                top = 5;
```

Example This program evaluates the polynomial $x^3 - 7.8x^2 + 18.5x - 11.3$ as the user enters the values of x. Notice the interesting way of evaluating the polynomial, and the balancing of brackets in the expression for p:

```
program polly;
  {Evaluate polynomial at points
   entered by the user}
  const a=1;
        b=-7.8;
        c=18.5;
        d=-11.3;
  var p,x:real;
  begin
    repeat
      write('Enter x ');
      read(x);
      p:=d+x*(c+x*(b+a*x));
      writeln(' polynomial p(x) is ',p)
    until false
  end.
```

8 The form of programs revisited

The programs seen so far consist of a single block of the form

declarations;
actions.

The declaration part consists of these elements which must be in the correct order:

program	(compulsory, must be first)
const	(optional, defines constants)
var	(optional, defines variable names)

Type and **label** declarations also exist and are described in later chapters.

The action part consists of

> **begin**
> > *statements*
> **end**.

Remember: blanks, newlines or comments act as separators, as do special symbols, like * in an expression. The semicolon separates statements and/or declarations from each other.

9 Standard functions for real values

A number of functions are provided for convenience which are mainly mathematical. For example, to find a square root it would be inconvenient for a programmer to have to agonize about the best way of doing this, when it has all been worked out long ago. Simply write

> *sqrt (value)*

as part of an expression, and the square root of the *value* will be found.

Here is a list of functions which give a real result based on the real or integer value x, which is called the *parameter* of the function.

abs(x)	absolute value, i.e. x made positive.
sqr(x)	the square of x, x^2.
sin(x)	the sine of x where x is in radians.
cos(x)	the cosine of x where x is in radians.
exp(x)	e to the power x; e is the base of natural logarithms.
ln(x)	natural logarithm of x. x must be > 0.
sqrt(x)	positive square root of x. x must be $>= 0$.
arctan(x)	the angle whose tangent is x; result in range $-\pi$ to π radians.

Actually *abs* and *sqr* will give an integer result if their parameter is an integer.

> *Example* A good way of evaluating π is to know that $\tan(\pi/4) = 1$, so that π is $4*arctan(1.0)$:

```
program pie;
  begin
    write('According to your computer the value of pi is ');
    writeln(4.0*arctan(1.0):20:15)
  end.
```

Running this program will demonstrate that real functions, like real numbers, do not have unlimited precision.

Example It is perhaps perverse of Pascal not to have an operator for raising to a power. Squaring can be done with *sqr*. Here is how to raise a real value to a real power:

$$value^{power} \qquad \text{is } exp(power * ln(value))$$

In the polynomial program, this could have been written:

p:= a*exp(3*ln(x)) + b*exp(2*ln(x)) + c*x + d

but it would not read well and be less efficient than

p:= d + x*(c+x*(b+a*x))

Computers multiply and add easily; they evaluate functions more slowly.

Two more functions using real parameters but giving integer results are *trunc(x)* and *round(x)* which are discussed near the end of the next chapter.

10 Problems

Problem 3.1 Write a density finding program, which prompts you for the mass and volume of an object and then tells you its density:

$$density = mass/volume$$

Problem 3.2 Write a program to find speed, which asks for a distance and also a time in hours, minutes and seconds. Look up the current world record for your favourite distance. How fast is the record holder moving?

$$speed = distance/time$$

Problem 3.3 From a standing start, the distance you cover in a given time at a constant rate of acceleration is

$$distance = \tfrac{1}{2}\ acceleration \times time^{2}$$

Write programs to answer these questions:

(i)   If you accelerate at a given rate, what distance do you cover in a given time?
(ii)   What acceleration is required to reach a given distance in a given time?
(iii) How long does it take to cover a given distance at a particular rate of acceleration?

Four
Working with integers

1 Integer constants and expressions

There are two basic ways of representing numbers in Pascal, by using the real type or the integer type. Reals can take a wide range of values but are limited in their accuracy. Integers, on the other hand, are exact but their range is limited. You can't have it both ways. The arithmetic of integers is the same as for reals except for division, as will be seen.

An integer constant is written without a decimal point. These are some constants:

Integer	Real	
3	3.Ø	6.Øe−12
−1Ø92	−1Ø.92	3e+1Ø
31416	3.1416	

In a **const** declaration the type is implied:

```
const
  one=1;
  two=2.Ø;
  biggie=3e1Ø;
  power1Ø=1Ø24;
```

Here, *one* and *power10* are integer constants; *two* and *biggie* are reals.

A special constant *maxint* is pre-declared in Pascal so that the range of integers available on a computer can be discovered by a program:

```
program findmax;
  begin
    writeln('Maxint on this computer is ',maxint)
  end.
```

All integers between −*maxint* and *maxint* will be available to a Pascal program.

Exercise Discover *maxint* on your computer. Is it really the largest integer?—try writing *maxint*+1. Is −*maxint* really the largest negative integer?—try writing −*maxint*−1.

In integer arithmetic, addition, subtraction and multiplication present no problems:

3+4	is 7	integer result
9−23	is −14	integer result
5*5	is 25	integer result

These results are of type *integer* because the terms involved are both integers. Mixing integers with reals is discussed at the end of this chapter.

Now for division. The expression

7/5	is 1.4	which is a real result

This may come as a surprise. The symbol / in Pascal is used to indicate a real division. The result is real even if the terms are integer. To get an integer result use the operator **div**:

7 **div** 5	is 1	integer result
−12 **div** 5	is −2	integer result

div is a dyadic operator which gives an integer division. The operands must be integers, and the result is an integer. The result is the same as doing a real division and then removing the decimal places, as the above examples show.

Another very useful operator related to integer division is **mod**, which gives the remainder after integer division.

7 **mod** 5	is 2	integer result
−12 **mod** 5	is −2	integer result

It may help the mathematically minded to define integer division and **mod** as follows:

$$number = (number \ \textbf{div} \ base) * base + number \ \textbf{mod} \ base$$

or, alternatively, *number* **mod** *base* is the same as

$$number - (number \ \textbf{div} \ base) * base$$

To understand expressions fully, the priority of **div** and **mod** has to be specified:

highest	( )	expressions in brackets
	* / **div mod**	multiplication and division
lowest	+ −	addition and subtraction

Operations of equal priority are carried out from left to right:

8 **div** 4 **mod** 3	is 2
8 **div** (4 **mod** 3)	is 8

2 Integer variables and assignment

Not surprisingly, variables can be declared in the **var** declaration:

```
var
  x,y:real;
  alpha,beta:integer;
```

In an assignment statement, a value can be assigned to an integer variable:

variable:=*expression*

For now the *expression* will be an integer one.

Example This program counts forever using an integer counter *counter*:

```
program intcount;
  var counter:integer;
  begin
    counter:=1;
    repeat
      writeln(counter);
      counter:=counter+1;
    until false
  end.
```

It would be very convenient to stop the *counter* at a particular value. The simplest way is to use a different form of **until**. **Repeat** . . . **until** is one of the structured statements of Pascal, which are discussed fully in Chapter 7. In the meantime, here is how to stop the *counter* at 10:

```
program stopatten;
  var counter:integer;
  begin
    counter:=1;
    repeat
      writeln(counter);
      counter:=counter+1;
    until counter=11
  end.
```

Exercise It is also very easy to count backwards. Do it.

3 Some interesting integer calculations

Most newcomers to computing see the obvious uses of real calculations, but many interesting and useful things that can be done with integers escape them. In this section some examples show the versatility of the **div** and **mod** operators, and in the next section some related applications are demonstrated in which the decimal places of real values are deliberately thrown away.

Example Pascal works with decimal numbers—the ones humans are most used to. The decimal number 461 is interpreted as follows:

4	6	1
hundreds	tens	units

Decimal numbers use the base ten. Other bases are possible; for example base 8:

7	1	5
sixty-fours	eights	units

In fact these two numbers are the same because

$$7 * 64 + 1 * 8 + 5 = 461$$

A decimal number can be converted to another base. The units part of a number in base 8 is

number **mod** 8   for example   461 **mod** 8 = 5

and   number **div** 8   is also needed,   461 **div** 8 = 57

The eights part is now

(number **div** 8) **mod** 8   for example   57 **mod** 8 = 1

To convert a number, re-use the **div** from each step; this is an iteration which is carried out until nothing is left:

461 **mod** 8 = 5	461 **div** 8 = 57
57 **mod** 8 = 1	57 **div** 8 = 7
7 **mod** 8 = 7	7 **div** 8 = 0 (finished)

The result 715 is read off backwards from the remainders. Here is a program which will convert a decimal number to any base using this method:

```
program anybase;

   {Converts a decimal number
    to any other base.}

   var number,base:integer;

   begin
     writeln('Program to convert a number to any base');
     write('Enter the number ..');
     readln(number);
     write('Enter the base ..');
     readln(base);
```

```
{Iterate until no digits are left}

repeat
  writeln('Here''s a digit',number mod base);
  number:=number div base;
until number=∅
end.
```

Exercise Make a program to convert a number from any base which is 10 or less to any other base. To do this, the input value, which Pascal thinks is decimal, has to be converted to the intended decimal value before being converted again to the new base.

Example A calendar date is made up of a day number and a month. The months are irregular in length. Consider how to work out the number of days since the beginning of the year. If all the months were 28 days long, it would be easy:

```
daynumber:=28*(month-1)+day
```

where the date is known by its day and month number from 1 (January) to 12 (December). Unfortunately the lengths of the months are irregular, and the dreaded February actually changes its length sometimes. To get around the February problem, use a fake month number which puts March at the beginning of the year. The table shows the total extra days to the beginning of the month to correct the error caused by pretending that each month has 28 days:

Number	Month	Days	Total extras
1	March	31	0
2	April	30	3
3	May	31	5
4	June	30	8
5	July	31	10
6	August	31	13
7	September	30	16
8	October	31	18
9	November	30	21
10	December	31	23
11	January	31	26
12	February	usually 28	29

The number of days counting from last March 1 is

```
frommarch:=day+28*(fakemonth-1)+extras
```

The clever part comes in getting the *fakemonth* and the *extras*. The *fakemonth* is

```
fakemonth:=1+(month+9) mod 12
```

and the total *extras* come from Zeller's congruence which is named after the person who proposed it:

```
extras:=(13*fakemonth-1) div 5 - 2
```

All of that will work for either normal years or leap years. For a normal 365 day year, the *daynumber* is the number of days counted from last March 1 plus 59 and less 365 if the month is January or February.

```
daynumber:=daysfrommarch+59-365*(fakemonth div 11)
```

So here is a program which computes the *daynumber* as long as the year is not a leap year:

```
program calendar;

  {Compute the day number from
   the date given as day and month}

  var day,month,
      fakemonth,
      daynumber,
      frommarch,
      extras,
      janorfeb : integer;

  begin
    write('Enter a date, first the day ..');
    readln(day);
    write('Now give the month number 1 to 12 ..');
    readln(month);

    {Count months frm March}

    fakemonth:=1 + (month+9) mod 12;

    {Zellers's congruence gives extras}

    extras:= (13*fakemonth-1) div 5 -2;
    frommarch:=day+28*(fakemonth-1)+extras;

    {Correct if January or February}

    janorfeb:=fakemonth div 11;
    daynumber:=frommarch+59-365*janorfeb;

    writeln('The day number is',daynumber)
  end.
```

Particularly notice the use of **div** and **mod**—that is the point of this example.

Exercise Compute the number of whole weeks and extra days left over since the beginning of the year—**div** and **mod** again.

4 Mixing reals and integers

In Pascal the good news is that an integer can always be used in place of a real, and the results will be as expected. The bad news is that a real value cannot be used where Pascal expects an integer. Some examples will illustrate these rules.

Examples An integer may always be used in place of a real.

(i) In expressions

$$3/4$$

Real division using one or two integer values will produce a real result, 0.75 in this case.

In general, if an operation has a real operand, a real value will be produced.

$$1.5 + 2 \qquad \text{has the real result 3.5.}$$

This implies that an expression with a real anywhere in it will turn out a real result unless it is deliberately converted back to an integer using the *trunc* or *round* functions introduced soon.

(ii) As parameters of functions

Sqrt(2.0) and *sqrt*(2) both give the same real result. Two functions are slightly special; *abs* and *sqr*. Both give a result which is real if the parameter is real and integer if the parameter is integer.

$$abs(-3) \qquad \text{is the integer value 3.}$$
$$abs(-3.0) \qquad \text{is the real value 3.0.}$$

(iii) In input

$$read \ (variable)$$

If the *variable* is either real or integer, an integer constant can be given.

(iv) Assignment

$$variable := expression$$

The *expression* can be integer if the *variable* is either real or integer.

Examples A real may not be used if an integer is expected.

(i) In expressions

The operands of **div** and **mod** must be integer. It is wrong to write 3.5 div 4.5 or *i* **mod** *j* unless both *i* and *j* are integers

(ii) As parameters of functions

Some functions expect integer parameters, for example *trunc* and *round*. Real values cannot be used as parameters of such functions.

(iii) In input

> *read* (*variable*)

If the *variable* is integer, an integer constant must be given. It is an error to give a value which has a decimal point, or an exponent.

(iv) Assignment

> *variable*:=*expression*

If the *variable* is an integer, the *expression* must give an integer result. It is an error to use a real *expression*. *Round* or *trunc* can be used to convert, as discussed next.

A programmer will often want to convert a real result to an integer. In doing this, the fractional part can either be thrown away, or used in rounding. Two functions convert a real value to an integer one:

trunc(*x*)   gives a 'truncated' result with the fractional part of *x* stripped away.

> *trunc*(3.5) is 3   *trunc*(−3.6) is −3

round(*x*)   gives the nearest integer to *x*.

> *round*(3.4) is 3   *round*(3.4999) is 3
> *round*(3.5) is 4   *round*(−3.6) is −4

Example The *trunc* function can be used to separate the whole and fractional parts of a real value. Using 3.14 as an example,

> *trunc*(3.14)

gives the integer value 3, and the fractional part can be recovered as

> 3.14 − *trunc*(3.14)

which provides the real value 0.14.

Using this idea, here is a program which takes a real distance in *kilometres* and converts it to *miles*, *yards*, *feets* and *inches*. There are 1.60934 *kilometres* in a *mile*. Given the *kilometres*, the *wholemiles* and the *fraction* left over can be computed from

```
miles:=kilometres/1.60935;
wholemiles:=trunc(miles);
fraction:=miles-wholemiles;
```

The *fraction* can then be made into *yards* and the process continued in a similar way:

```
    program metric;

    {Convert real kilometres to miles, yards,
       feet and inches rounded to Ø.1 inches}

      var kilometres,miles,
          yards,feets,
          inches,fraction:real;
          wholemiles,wholeyards,
          wholefeets:integer;

      begin
        write('Enter distance in kilometres ..');
        readln(kilometres);
        miles:=kilometres/1.6Ø934;
        wholemiles:=trunc(miles);
        fraction:=miles-wholemiles;
        yards:=fraction*176Ø;
        wholeyards:=trunc(yards);
        fraction:=yards-wholeyards;
        feets:=fraction*3;
        wholefeets:=trunc(feets);
        fraction:=feets-wholefeets;
        inches:=12*fraction;
        inches:=round(inches*1Ø)/1Ø;
        write('Answer: ',wholemiles,' miles, ');
        write(wholeyards,' yards, ',wholefeets,' feet, ');
        writeln(inches:5:2,' inches')
      end.
```

Notice that *inches* in the example are actually rounded to the nearest 0.1 inch, by scaling them, rounding them, and then undoing the scale. This technique can also be used in truncation. To take a sum of money expressed in dollars down to the next lowest cent, do this:

```
      payout:=trunc(money*1ØØ)/1ØØ
```

(A famous computer fraud consisted of crediting account holders with their interest after it had been truncated, while crediting the criminal with the tiny fractions of cents left over. Done often to thousands of accounts, this was a lot of money!)

Exercise Write a program to convert a real time in hours into hours, minutes and seconds. For example 18.5 hours is 18 hours, 30 minutes and no seconds.

5 Writing out integers

In the metric conversion example, the spacing of the output has been left to the computer. It is possible to have

      write(*integervalue*:*digits*)   {or *writeln*}

where *digits* is an integer greater than zero telling the computer how many spaces to use in displaying the integer value. If digits is not large enough, the computer will decide what to do. In the metric example, *wholeyards* cannot be more than four digits, and *wholefeets* can only be one digit. Therefore the output is more pleasing if these statements are used:

```
write('Answer: ',wholemiles:3,' miles, ');
write(wholeyards:4,' yards, ',wholefeets:1,' feet, ');
writeln(inches:5:2,' inches')
```

6 Functions for integer values

The functions mainly used to produce integer results are *trunc* and *round*, introduced above.

trunc(x)   truncates its real or integer parameter x to an integer result.

round(x)   rounds its real or integer parameter x to an integer result.

These functions, given here for reference, also give integer results:

ord(x)   if x is an integer the result is the integer value x. This function is useful in processing characters as described in Chapter 13, and also for enumerated or subrange types introduced in Chapter 15.

pred(x)   is $x-1$ if x is an integer. Useful with other data types—it means predecessor.

succ(x)   is $x+1$ if x is an integer. Useful with other data types—it means successor.

These functions, given here for reference, require an integer parameter:

odd(x)   is a function whose result is of type *boolean* (Chapter 5). It is *true* if x is an odd number, *false* otherwise. The parameter x must be an integer.

chr(x)   is a function whose result is the character whose order in the computer's character sequence is x (Chapter 13). The parameter must be an integer.

ord(*chr*(x))   is x and   *chr*(*ord*(*ch*))   is *ch* where *ch* is of type *char*.

7 Problems

Problem 4.1 In 1971 the British currency system was changed from real money:

> one pound   = 20 shillings
> one shilling = 12 pence (pennies)
> one penny   = 4 farthings (farthings disappeared many years ago.)

to the rather colourless modern one:

one pound (now a chocolate coin) = 100 new pence (or 'nuppence')

Write a program to convert chocolate money to real money. Write a program to convert real money to chocolate money.

Problem 4.2 Fermat's Last Theorem states that there are no integer solutions other then 0 to

$$x^n + y^n = z^n$$

for $n > 2$. Various proofs have been claimed, and no-one has ever found a solution which disproves it. So don't waste your time trying to find a solution of

$$x^3 + y^3 = z^3$$

Instead, find all the integer right angled triangles

$$a^2 + b^2 = h^2$$

with hypotenuse $h < 100$. For example,

$$3^2 + 4^2 = 5^2$$

is a solution known and used since ancient times. Do not use any Pascal features which have not yet been covered.

Problem 4.3 1 March 1600 was a Wednesday. By counting the days from then, work out the day of the week for any Gregorian date. (The Gregorian calendar is the one used nearly everywhere.) To do this, the number of leap years has to be taken into account. Everyone knows that an extra day is put into February if the year is divisible by 4—that is how a leap year is defined. But an exact century is not a leap year unless it is divisible by 400 — 1900 was but 2000 will not be. This is all done by **div** and **mod**.

Problem 4.4 Working out the date of Easter is quite a tricky business. By decision of the Council of Nicea in 325, Easter is celebrated on the Sunday immediately following the first full moon which occurs on or after March 21. Being unaware of the earth's rotation, they thought that midnight occurred simultaneously everywhere, whereas in fact a full moon could occur on 20 March in Rome, near midnight, when it was aready 21 March in Jerusalem. This could create a month's uncertainty in the date of Easter. Unfortunately, the Church does not apply actual astronomical data to this rule to calculate the date of Easter. Rather, a formula was devised and has been applied blindly ever since. I telephoned the Royal Greenwich Observatory to get the data for this problem and they told me that their (highly scientific) method for predicting the date of Easter was to look in the Book of Common Prayer.

However, the moon was full on Friday, 5 October 1979 at 35.32 minutes past 19:00 Greenwich mean time, and the mean period for the moon's phases can be taken as 29.53059 days.

Devise a method for computing the Gregorian date of Easter for any year, assuming the critical observations are based on Greenwich mean time. To do this, work out the phase of the moon at 00:00 GMT on 21 March, move forward to the next full moon and then move forward to the next Sunday. Recently, Easter was held on the wrong date according to these calculations. When?

Five
Decisions

1 Boolean constants, variables and expressions

Boolean algebra is the mathematical description of logic, named after George Boole (1815—1864) who developed many of the concepts involved. It is of fundamental importance in designing the circuitry of computers and also in describing the decisions that programs can make. Pascal uses the *boolean* type which has two values—*true* and *false*. Therefore *true* and *false* are the two constants that are available. Although it has not yet been fully described, the structure

>   repeat
>   *statements*
>   until *false*

contains the boolean constant *false*, and has been used several times in earlier chapters.

Constants of type *boolean* can be given names in a **const** declaration, although this is of limited value since there are only two values available:

```
const yes=true;
      no=false;
```

This might be an amusing approach to the endless repetition that has been used:

```
program eternal;
  const eternity=false;
  begin
    repeat
      write('Stop me .. ')
    until eternity
  end.
```

Variables of type *boolean* can be used:

```
var finished:boolean;
```

Boolean expressions use the operators **not**, **and**, and **or**, which must have operands of type *boolean*.

Not is a unary operator which negates or changes a boolean value:

>   **not** *true*   is *false*
>   **not** *false*   is *true*

The **and** operation is dyadic, and gives a *true* result if both its operands are *true, false* otherwise. This is a truth table describing the **and** operation:

false **and** *false*	is *false*
false **and** *true*	is *false*
true **and** *false*	is *false*
true **and** *true*	is *true*

The dyadic **or** operation has a *true* result if either operand is *true*. It is also *true* if both operands are *true* and is often called the 'inclusive' **or** because it includes this case. Its truth table is:

false **or** *false*	is *false*
false **or** *true*	is *true*
true **or** *false*	is *true*
true **or** *true*	is *true*

As with arithmetic, the priority of these operations is important:

not	*highest*
and	
or	*lowest*

Not has been given the highest priority in Pascal, unlike some other languages in which it has the lowest priority. Any negated boolean expression in Pascal must be bracketed, and as this often seems unnatural, it is a source of programming errors.

Examples

not *true* **and** *false*	is *false*
not (*true* **and** *false*)	is *true*

Mixing these with other operations will be seen in the next section.

These are three functions in Pascal which give *boolean* results:

odd(x) x must be an integer. *Odd(x)* is *true* if x is an odd number, i.e. if $abs(x)$ **mod** $2 = 1$.

eof(file) is *true* if no further information can be read from the file. See Chapters 13 and 17. Just putting *eof* with no parameter refers to the normal input file. See Chapters 13 and 17.

eoln(file) is *true* if no further information can be obtained from the current line of a file. Just putting *eoln* without a parameter refers to the normal input file. See Chapters 13 and 17.

Example The logical operations *nand* (**not and**) and *nor* (**not or**) are not basic operations in Pascal, but are very important in the design of logic circuits. They are easily achieved. If *a* and *b* are boolean values, then

```
nor:=not(a or b)
nand:=not(a and b)
```

would evaluate the *nor* and *nand* of *a* with *b*.

Exercise In a Pascal program, construct truth tables for *nor* and *nand*. What would happen if the brackets were omitted from the above expressions?

2 Making comparisons with relational expressions

A relational expression compares two values and gives a result which is *true* or *false*, of type *boolean*. This is the basis of decision making. Consider the program *stopatten*:

```
program stopatten;
  var counter:integer;
  begin
    counter:=1;
    repeat
      writeln(counter);
      counter:=counter+1;
    until counter=11
  end.
```

Here, the counting is repeated until the *relational expression counter*=11 is *true*.

A *relational expression* is

> *value   relational operator   value*

The values compared must be of the same type except that an integer can always be compared with a real. Comparisons with characters are considered in Chapter 13, and the situation for other types is clarified where they are introduced.

The available *relational operators* are

=	equal
<>	not equal
<	less than
>	greater than
<=	less or equal (different meaning for sets; see Chapter 15)
>=	greater or equal (different meaning for sets; see Chapter 15)
in	(only used with sets; see Chapter 15)

Of the types studied so far, integers and reals can be compared using any relational operator. However reals are approximate values and so a program which expects an exact equality with reals is likely not to work correctly. It would be surprising if

$$.63=.7*(.63/.7)$$

were true, even though mathematically it should be. In Chapter 7 the unsuitability of reals for counting will be discussed.

Boolean values can also be compared. In Pascal, *false* is considered to have a value less than *true*—the reason for this is revealed in Chapter 16—but it is unlikely that real people will want to use boolean values in such a confusing way.

Example The power series for sin x is

$$\sin x = x - \frac{x^3}{3!} + \frac{x^5}{5!} - \frac{x^7}{7!} + \ldots$$

This program evaluates sin x, not by using the *sin* function but by summing this power series until the last term is less than 10^{-4}. The iteration is stopped by the decision

```
until abs(term) <= 1e-4
```

```
program sinesum;
  var x,sum,term:real;
      power:integer;
  begin
    writeln('Evaluates power series for sine x');
    write('Enter a value for x .. ');
    readln(x);
    {Initialize the sum}
    sum:=x;
    term:=x;
    power:=1;
    writeln('  Power        Term           Sum');
    writeln(power:5,term:15:6,sum:15:6);
    {Do the iteration}
    repeat
      power:=power+2;
      term:=-term*x*x/power/(power-1);
      sum:=sum + term;
      writeln(power:5,term:15:6,sum:15:6);
    until abs(term) <= 1e-4
  end.
```

This program uses what is called a *recurrence* to compute each term in the series from the one before it. It is easy to see in the power series formula that for a given power

$$term_{power} = -term_{power-2} * \frac{x^2}{(power)(power-1)}$$

Exercise As x increases, the number of terms required to complete the power series also increases. Because sin x repeats every time x goes through 2π radians, any value of x can be reduced to an equivalent value in the range $-\pi<=x<=\pi$. Make the program do this—it is a simple calculation—and find the maximum number of terms now required to compute sin x.

These new relational and logical operators might be combined with each other, or even with the operators of arithmetic, in reaching decisions. This requires the priority of all operations to be defined, which is:

( )	expressions in brackets
not	
* / **div mod and**	(operators like multiplication)
+ − **or**	(operators like addition or signs)
relational operators	

In making an expression, remember that boolean operators can only operate on boolean terms, and arithmetic operators can only operate on real or integer terms. A relational operator will always produce a boolean result. So an expression with a relational operator in it is going to turn out boolean in the end.

Example The expression

$$\textbf{not } 2+1>5 \textbf{ or } 2$$

is a disaster because it asks for the impossible operations **not** 2 and **or** 2. The programmer who wrote this might have intended

$$\textbf{not } (2+1>5) \textbf{ or } (2+1>2) \qquad \text{which is true}$$

or

$$\textbf{not } ((2+1>5) \textbf{ or } (2+1>2)) \qquad \text{which is false}$$

Look at these carefully.

3 Decisions with the if statement

The **if** statement is one of the most general ways of making decisions in a computer program:

if *booleanvalue* **then** *statement*

When this occurs, the *booleanvalue* is worked out and the *statement* is executed if the result was *true*. Here we see a statement written within a statement.

Example In Pascal a *write* or *writeln* statement will display a boolean value in some manner on a screen or terminal. You can state an optional field width:

```
write (true:8)
```

However *read* and *readln* cannot accept a boolean value which is entered from the keyboard. To do this you have to use an integer with an **if** statement. In this example, *thing* is set to *false* if 0 is entered, but is *true* if anything else is given. After Chapter 13, where characters are considered, it will be just as easy to use F and T (or N and Y).

```
program iffy;
  {Shows how to define and display
    boolean values}
  var thing:boolean;
      input:integer;
  begin
    repeat
      write('Enter an integer, 0 for false .. ');
      readln(input);
      {Define it here}
      thing:=true;
      if input=0 then thing:=false;
      {And now display it}
      writeln('You gave me ',thing)
    until false
  end.
```

Very often, in making a decision, the choice is between two alternatives, and that is the purpose of the **if** . . . **then** . . . **else** construction:

> **if** *booleanvalue* **then** *truestatement* **else** *falsestatement*

The *truestatement* is taken if the *booleanvalue* is *true*, and the *falsestatement* is taken otherwise.

Here is a program which evaluates the boolean function for 'exclusive or', which is not included in Pascal as an operation but which is easily simulated. If *a* and *b* are boolean values, then the exclusive or is like **or**, except that it is *false* when *a* and *b* are both *true*. It is easily seen, for example by writing a truth table, that

```
eor:=(a and not b) or (b and not a)

program piglet;

  {Simulate the exclusive or operation}

  var a,b,eor:boolean;
      ina,inb:integer;
  begin
    repeat
      writeln;
      write('Enter two values, 0 is false .. ');
      readln(ina,inb);
      if ina=0 then a:=false else a:=true;
      if inb=0 then b:=false else b:=true;

      {Echo the given values}

      write('You gave me a = ',a);
      writeln(' and b = ',b);
```

```
{work out and display a EOR b}

eor:=(a and not b) or (b and not a);
writeln('The exclusive OR of these is ',eor);
    until false
end.
```

Exercise Write a program to find and display the larger of two real values entered. Read in two real values, and assign the larger value to a variable *big*. This can be done with or without **else**, and without **else** it can use either one or two if statements. Which of these alternatives do you prefer?

4 Compound statements

After a decision, the action to be taken is most often not a single statement, but a series. In Pascal the compound statement can be used anywhere that a statement is called for. **Begin** and **end** are used to delimit a compound statement:

> **begin** *statement*; *statement* . . .; *statement* **end**

Therefore the action part of a Pascal program is itself a compound statement.

Example Given two numbers, *first* and *second*, this program puts them in order so that *second* is the larger. This is done by switching the values if necessary. Notice that the actual switch takes three statements using a temporary variable *save*. Why is this necessary?

```
program order;
  var first,second,save:real;
  begin
    write('Enter two real values .. ');
    readln(first,second);
    if first>second then
      {Here is the compound statement}
      begin
        writeln('Re-ordering those values');
        save:=first; first:=second; second:=save
      end;
    writeln('In order now ',first,second)
  end.
```

Indenting the statements inside compound statements makes the structure of programs easier to follow. Indentation is not necessary—it is just vital because it makes things clearer.

5 Problems

Problem 5.1 Write a program which puts three numbers into increasing order. Do not anticipate Pascal facilities which are introduced later.

Problem 5.2 Write a program which finds the largest of four numbers. Do not anticipate Pascal facilities which are introduced later.

Problem 5.3 Write a program to play against you, a simplified version of the game NIMB. The game begins with 15 objects on a table. Each of the two players in turn must remove one, two, or three objects. The loser is the player forced to remove the last one. Make your program always win if given the first move, and also win if the human player blunders even if given the first move. The winning stategy has **mod** in it and is very simple if you know it.

Problem 5.4 Write a program to find the greatest common divisor of two given integers. The elegant solution has **mod** in it (of course) and is called Euclid's algorithm. See if you can rediscover it.

Six
Some basics summarized

The previous chapters have introduced some basic elements of the Pascal language which are summarized here. Be sure they are well understood before going on.

1 Basic types

Pascal has four basic types of data: *real*, *integer*, *boolean* and *char* (meaning character). The *char* type is introduced in Chapter 13. A Pascal program can also define its own types, as discussed in Chapter 15.

Real values represent numbers over a wide range of values and include fractional values to some limit of precision which depends on the computer. Integer values represent whole numbers over a more limited range than reals, and are exact. An integer value can always be given in place of a real one.

Boolean values can be *true* or *false*.

2 Identifiers

An identifier begins with a letter and then contains any mixture of letters and numbers. It cannot contain other symbols.

Correct	Incorrect
Identifier	*1Zoom*
Splat123	*First — last*
Noblankseither	*No blanks either*

A capital letter means the same as the corresponding small letter:

> *BigBug* is the same as *bigbug*

Pascal should allow identifiers of any length, and all the symbols should be significant even in long names. Not all implementations follow this rule.

> *JohnandMarySmith*   should be different from
> *JohnandMaryJones*   —but don't count on it.

A number of names which are keywords of Pascal cannot be used as identifiers. These are

and	**do**	**function**	**nil**	**program**	**type**
array	**downto**	**goto**	**not**	**record**	**until**
begin	**else**	**if**	**of**	**repeat**	**var**
case	**end**	**in**	**or**	**set**	**while**
const	**file**	**label**	**packed**	**then**	**with**
div	**for**	**mod**	**procedure**	**to**	

Any other name can be used.

An identifier can name a type, constant, variable, function, procedure, file or directive. A number of these are predefined, but a program could take them over for some other use. This would usually be very bad style. Here is a list of predefined identifiers:

types	*boolean char integer real*
constants	*false maxint true*
variables	*input*∧ *output*∧
functions	*abs arctan chr cos eof eoln exp ln*
	ord pred round sin sqr sqrt succ trunc odd
procedures	*get reset rewrite put* (Chapters 17, 18)
	read readln write writeln (Chapter 2)
	dispose new (Chapter 18)
	pack unpack (Chapter 15)
files	*input output* (Chapter 17)
directives	*external forward* (Chapter 9)

3 Constants

An integer constant is written as a whole number with no decimal point, for example

    23   −1Ø24   +34

Maxint is a predefined integer constant. All integer values from −*maxint* to *maxint* will be available on a particular computer.

A real constant is written in one of two forms, either as a number with decimal places, for example

    3.1416   −6.23   +1.Ø

or in scientific notation with a signed integer exponent:

$$number \quad \begin{matrix} e \\ or \\ E \end{matrix} \quad signed\ exponent$$

such as

    3e+1Ø   6.525e−27

A string constant is any series of symbols enclosed in single quotes. To include a single quote, put two of them.

A constant of one of the basic types can be given a name in a **const** declaration. The type is implied in the declaration.

> **const** *identifier = value*;
>   *identifier = value*;
>   .
>   .
>   .

For example,

```
const oneint=1;
      onereal=1.Ø;
      eternity=false;
```

Here *oneint* is the name of the integer constant 1, while *onereal* is real—the decimal place in its declaration makes it real.

4 Variables

Variables are used to hold values which can be defined and manipulated by a program. A variable has a name, a type and a value. The name and type must be declared in a **var** declaration.

> **var** *identifier, identifier . . ., identifier:type*;
>   *identifier, identifier . . ., identifier:type*;

The value of a variable is undefined when the action part of a program begins. It is wrong to expect it to have a value until the program has defined it. A value can be defined by assignment or by reading it from a file. This could occur in a procedure (such as *readln*) or even a function.

5 Expressions

An expression combines values using operations whose results are new values.

> *operand   operator   operand*

Between real or integer values the following operations can be used:

+	addition
−	subtraction
*	multiplication
/	division

The result of these operations is real if either operand was real, otherwise both operands are integer and the result is integer. This implies that a numerical expression with a real in it anywhere will turn out real.

The following operations can be used between integers only, and produce an integer result:

> **div** truncated division
> **mod** remainder

The following operations can be done between boolean values only:

> **and**
> **or**

These operations are monadic, taking one operand only:

> **not** boolean value
> $+$ real or integer value
> $-$ real or integer value

The relational operations can be done between any values of the same type, recalling that an integer can always be substituted for a real:

> $=$ equal
> $<$ not equal
> $<$ less than
> $>$ greater than
> $<=$ less than or equal (different meaning for sets; see Chapter 15)
> $>=$ greater than or equal (different meaning for sets; see Chapter 15)
> **in**   (only used with sets; see Chapter 15)

The boolean value *false* is less than *true*.

See Chapter 7 for comments on comparing real values for equality.

The priority of all operations is:

> ( )   expressions in brackets
> **not**
> * / **div mod and**   (operators like multiplication)
> $+$ $-$ **or**   (operators like addition or signs)
> *relational operators*

6 Programs

A Pascal program consists of:

> *declarations*;
> *action*.

The first declaration must identify the program:

> *program identifier* (*file names*);
>
> if external files are used (see Chapter 17)

The remaining declarations must appear in the correct order:

> **label** (Chapter 7)
>
> **const**
> **var**
> **type**
>
> **procedure**   (Chapter 9)   or **function**   (Chapter 11)

The *action* consists of a compound statement:

> **begin**
>   *statement*;
>   *statement*;
>
>   .
>   .
>   .
>
>   *statement*
> **end**

A period (or 'full stop') occurs at the end of the program.

Semicolons are used to separate complete statements from each other. Semicolons never occur before **else**. Semicolons never occur after **begin** or **then** or **else** or **repeat**. Why? Because these are not places where statements are separated.

Semicolons can be used before **end** or **until**. Why? See Chapter 8.

A comment is any series of symbols beginning with { or (* and ending with } or *), unless these are part of a string constant.

7 The statements of Pascal so far

The compound statement:

> **begin**
>   *statement*;
>   *statement*;
>
>   .
>   .
>   .
>
>   *statement*
> **end**

A reference to a **procedure** is a statement, for example

    writeln

The assignment statement:

> *variable*:=*expression*

The **repeat** . . . **until** statement:

> **repeat**
>   *statement*;
>   *statement*;
>
>   .
>   .
>   .
>
>   *statement*
> **until** *decision*

The **if** statement:

> **if** *decision* **then** *statement*

and with **else**:

> **if** *decision* **then** *statement* **else** *statement*

Seven
Looping and repeating

1 Repeat ... until

When part of a program is repeated over and over, it has become traditional to call the repeated statements a *loop*, and the process of repetition is often called *iteration*. These features of computer programming have already been demonstrated, for example in counting:

```
program stopatten;          repeat
  var counter:integer;         writeln(counter);
  begin                        counter:=counter+1
    counter:=1;             until counter=11
                          end.
```

Here, the iteration generates successive values of *counter* until the **until** condition becomes *true*.

Repeat . . . **until** is one of the structured statements of Pascal—the others are introduced in this chapter and the next. This is the definition of **repeat** . . . **until**:

> **repeat** *statement*; *statement* . . .; *statement* **until** *booleanvalue*

All the statements between **repeat** and **until** are repeated until the *booleanvalue* becomes *true*. The decision to repeat is made each time at the end of the structure, as demonstrated in this counting program. All of the values from 1 to 5 are printed even though the value of *finished* becomes *true* before the *writeln* statement:

```
program testatend;          repeat
  var counter:integer;         counter:=counter+1;
      finished:boolean;        if counter=5 then finished:=true;
  begin                        writeln('Counting ',counter)
    counter:=0;             until finished
    finished:=false;      end.
```

Example The factorial of an integer *n* is written as *n*! and defined by

$$n! = n(n-1)(n-2) \ldots 1$$

which can be obtained by an iteration which multiplies all the numbers from 1 to *n* together.

```
program factorial;
  var n,nshriek:integer;
  begin
    repeat
      write('Enter n to get its factorial ..');
      readln(n)
    until n>0;
    nshriek:=1;
    repeat
      nshriek:=nshriek*n;
      n:=n-1
    until n=0;
    writeln('The factorial is ',nshriek)
  end.
```

Notice how the program uses **repeat** . . . **until** in forcing a correct value of *n* to be entered.

Exercise The factorials of even modest integers can be very large. Use this program to discover the largest factorial that can be obtained using integers. Although the factorial is an integer concept, the range of real numbers is much larger. Modify the program so that the input is an integer but the result is real. Now how large can *n* be?

Example A prime number is an integer which has no factors other than itself and 1. This program tests *number* to see if it is prime. To do this, all the integers from 2 to *sqrt(number)* could be checked to see if they divide exactly into *number*. However, only half as much effort is needed if only odd numbers are accepted and odd factors are tried. Notice the use of the **mod** operation to test for a factor:

```
program prime;
  var number,test:integer;
      maybe:boolean;
  begin

    {Obtain the trial prime}

    repeat
      write('Enter an odd number > 3 to see if it is
        prime..');
      readln(number)
    until (number>3) and odd(number);

    {Test this number}

    test:=3;
    maybe:=true;
    repeat
      writeln('Testing',test);
      if number mod test = 0 then maybe:= false;
      test:=test+2
    until (maybe=false) or (test>sqrt(number)+1);
```

```
{Display the result}

if maybe then writeln('It is prime.')
   else writeln('It is not prime.')
end.
```

Two details are worth noticing in the **until** condition that ends the prime testing loop:

```
until (maybe=false) or (test>sqrt(number)+1)
```

The brackets around the terms separated by **or** are necessary because of the hierarchy of boolean operations, in which the **or** operator has a higher priority than comparisons. Take the brackets away, and the program becomes illegal because the operation

```
false or test
```

compares items of incompatible types. Secondly, the *sqrt* function cannot be relied upon to give exactly the square root of a perfect square like 25—the result of *sqrt* is real. It might give a real value slightly less than 5, in which case the program would stop on

```
test>sqrt(number)
```

without trying 5 as a factor! Remember that a real value is an approximation which might or might not be exact.

2 Testing first with while

A shrewd reader will have noticed that a **repeat** . . . **until** construction always runs through the loop once, because the **until** condition is checked at the end. It may be more convenient to test at the beginning, as in the **while** construction:

> **while** *booleanvalue* **do** *statement*

Although the **while** construction appears to contain only one statement, it would often be a compound statement, as in this example of yet another counting program:

```
program yetagain;                      begin
  var counter:integer;                   writeln(counter);
  begin                                  counter:=counter+1
    counter:=1;                        end
    while counter<11 do              end.
```

Endless iteration is also a rather neat structure using **while**:

```
program tiresome;
  begin
    while true do write('Ho—hum ..')
  end.
```

Example A factorial program was given in the previous section. The factorial of 0 should be 1, and this cannot be achieved nicely using **repeat**. How can it be improved? With **while**:

```
program factorial2;
  var n,nshriek:integer;
  begin
    repeat
      write('Enter n to get its factorial ..');
      readln(n)
    until n>=0;
    nshriek:=1;
    while n>1 do
      begin
        nshriek:=nshriek*n;
        n:=n-1
      end;
    writeln('The factorial is ',nshriek)
  end.
```

Observe how the cases $n=0$ and $n=1$ are handled by this program.

Exercise The number of ways of reordering (or permuting) n items is $n!$, calculated above. The number of permutations of n items taken in groups of r is called $_nP_r$ and is

$$_nP_r = n(n-1)(n-2) \ldots (n-r+1)$$

$$= \frac{n!}{(n-r)!}$$

Write a program to evaluate $_nP_r$. Do it both with **while** and with **repeat**.

3 About counting—the for statement

It is easy enough to count with integers as has been seen. Counting either up or down by 1 on each repetition is a common requirement, and that is why Pascal provides a special statement for this, the **for** statement:

> **for** *variable*:=*start* **to** *finish* **do** *statement*

or

> **for** *variable*:=*start* **downto** *finish* **do** *statement*

When this is executed, the *statement* is repeated with the index *variable* taking all the values between *start* and *finish*, counting up if **to** is used, or down if **downto** is used. The **for** structure is like **while** in the sense that it may not be done at all if the values of *start* and *finish* indicate that it should not.

Examples Suppose *counter* is an integer variable. This one is executed 10 times:

```
for counter:=1 to 10 do writeln(counter)
```

This one is not executed at all:

```
for counter:=2 to 1 do writeln(counter)
```

while this is done twice:

```
for counter:=2 downto 1 do writeln(counter)
```

The index variable used in a **for** statement must not be of real type—why this is sensible will be discussed shortly. We will find in Chapter 9 that in a procedure or function the index variable must be local. It can be of any simple type that takes a succession of values. These are called *ordinal types* in Pascal. The most obvious of them is the integer type, but the boolean type is also one, in which *true* comes after *false*:

```
program tryit;
  var booboo:boolean;
  begin
    for booboo:=false to true do writeln('See?')
  end.
```

This loop is repeated twice, the first time with *booboo=false* and the second time with *booboo=true*. The character type introduced in Chapter 13 is another example, as is any type created by the program which is a subrange of a simple ordinal type (Chapter 15) or an enumerated type (also Chapter 15). Here is a foretaste of the character type which displays all of the small letters a to z:

```
program alphabet;
  var letter:char;
  begin
    for letter:='a' to 'z' do write(letter)
  end.
```

In a **for** loop, the starting and finishing values must be correct for the type of variable being used to count. Within the loop, it is wrong to include any statement that could cause the counting variable to become changed. This program is illegal according to the Pascal standard although, just to complicate life, it works on my computer:

```
program illegal;                         begin
  var stupid:integer;                      writeln(stupid);
  begin                                    stupid:=stupid*2
    for stupid:=1 to 100 do              end
                                   end.
```

Inside a **for** structure, Pascal should not allow the index variable to be given a new value by an assignment statement, or by another **for** statement, or to be used as a variable parameter in any procedure or function reference—including *read* or *readln*. Just remember that the counting variable is sacred and therefore Pascal should not allow anything that either does change or could change its value. Even if a particular implementation of Pascal allows it, it is unwise because any program which conflicts with standard Pascal is not fully portable.

Finally, the value of the index variable is undefined after a **for** loop is fully completed. This program should fail because at the *writeln* statement, the variable silly is undefined. (On my computer it displays 6. So much for theory!)

```
program shouldfail;
  var silly:integer;
  begin
    for silly:=1 to 5 do begin end;
    writeln(silly)
  end.
```

Example The number of combinations of n things taken r at a time, called $_nC_r$, is found by removing the r reorderings of each choice from $_nP_r$:

$$_nC_r = \frac{n!}{(n-r)!\ r!}$$

One might be tempted to do this by calculating three factorials, but there is a much more efficient way. Observe that there is a recurrence:

$$_nC_r = \frac{n-r+1}{r}\ _nC_{r-1}$$

Because $_nC_0$ is 1, $_nC_r$ can be built up using this recurrence relationship. Not only is it more efficient, it is unlikely to produce impossibly large integers along the way and so will work for a wide range of the integers n and r. Although a minicomputer probably can't do the factorial of 8, this program has no trouble with $_8C_r$ for any value of r:

```
program combo;

  {Program to work out combinations nCr}

  var n,r,nCr,counter:integer;
  begin
    {Obtain correct n and r}

    writeln('This program computes nCr.');
    writeln;
    repeat
      write('Enter n and r, both integers >= 0 .. ');
      readln(n,r);
    until (n>=0) and (r>=0);

    {Compute nCr by recurrence from 1 to r}

    nCr:=1;    {nC0 is always 1}
    for counter:=1 to r do
      nCr:=(n-r+counter)*nCr div counter;
    writeln('Number of combinations is',nCr)
  end.
```

Exercise Develop a program which finds all the prime numbers which are less than some given maximum.

4 Why not count with reals?

Because a real value is only an approximation. This would not cause trouble while the counting is going on, but it always causes trouble in deciding when to stop. Reals are not exact, and therefore they should never be compared for equality. This is illegal because a real counter cannot be used in a **for** structure:

```
program hopeless;

   {This program is illegal}

   var realcount:real;
   begin
     for realcount:=0.1 to 1.0 do writeln(realcount)
   end.
```

Suppose a program wishes to count the 11 real values from 0.0 to 1.0 in steps of 0.1. There is only one safe way to do this—use an integer to count. But first the unsafe ways are demonstrated. This is a legal program, but it is not certain to work:

```
program danger;

   {This is a legal program
     but it will not stop counting}

   var realcount:real;

begin
  realcount:=0.0;
  repeat
    writeln(realcount:5:2);
    realcount:=realcount+0.1
  until realcount=1.0
end.
```

Why? Because the real value cannot be represented exactly in a digital computer, and therefore the exact value 1.0 will not be reached. The program could surge past the intended stopping place and go on forever.

Never rely on a real value to be exact!

The only safe procedure is to generate a real count from an integer one. This is how:

```
program safety;

   {Creates a real counter from an integer one}

   var realcount:real;
       intcount:integer;
   begin
     for intcount:= 0 to 10 do
       begin
         realcount:=intcount/10;
         writeln(realcount:5:2)
       end
   end.
```

5 About summation

Adding things up is one of the most important kinds of iteration. Counting is itself a form of summing, and this is very obvious if either the **repeat** or **while** structure is used:

```
program stopatten;
  var counter:integer;
  begin
    counter:=1;
    repeat
      writeln(counter);
      counter:=counter+1;
    until counter=11
  end.
```

Here, the *counter* is initialized before the loop, and within the loop it has 1 added to it each time. This is exactly what has to be done for any other kind of summation.

Example Sum the numbers from 1 to *n*. (This predicts how many presents will arrive on the *n*th day of Christmas.)

```
program greedy;

  {Twelve days of Xmas Mark I}

  var daynumber,sum,count:integer;
  begin

    {Find out the day number}

    writeln('Hello, greedy one. I''ll tell you how');
    writeln('many presents to expect on the Nth day');
    write('of Christmas. What is the day number? ..');
    readln(daynumber);

    {Initialize the sum}

    sum:=0;
    count:=1;

    {Add them up in this loop}

    while count<=daynumber do
      begin
        sum:=sum+count;
        count:=count+1
      end;

    {Report on the results}

    writeln('Today you can expect',sum,' prezzies.')
  end.
```

There is, of course, a formula for this.

Exercise Form the sum of sums from 1 to *n*. (This gives the total number of presents received on all the days of Christmas up to and including day *n*.)

6 The last resort—goto

Here is a horrible program which repeats forever:

```
program horrid;
  label 1Ø;
  begin
    1Ø: write('Stop me .. ');
        goto 1Ø
  end.
```

The **goto** statement alters the flow of a program by jumping to a labelled statement. Any labels used have to be declared in a **label** statement, which must always be the first declaration in a block (as was summarized in Chapter 6). A label is always a series of up to four digits which make it look like an integer in the range 0 to 9999. The **label** declaration is:

label *digits, digits . . ., digits*;

The only purpose of a **label** declaration is to specify the labels that **goto** statements will use. Notice that the **goto** keyword is one word—without a blank in the middle.

Using **goto** in a Pascal program is considered an admission of failure and is very much frowned upon. In Pascal, the structured statements are supposed to encourage well organized programs which are easy to understand. In some other computer languages, the widespread use of **goto** statements is blamed for the poorly organized and badly structured programs that are often written.

Occasionally in Pascal, a **goto** statement might add clarity, but it is never necessary. One acceptable use could be in escaping from the body of a structured statement. For example, the **while** statement checks for completion at the beginning of an iteration, and the **repeat** . . . **until** tests at the end. Occasionally it might be desirable to leave in the middle with a **goto** statement. This is the $_nC_r$ program again, but it is now organized to repeat itself until both *n* and *r* are 999:

```
program combotoo;

  {Another program to work out combinations nCr}

  label 1Ø;
  var n,r,nCr,counter:integer;
  begin
    repeat

    {Obtain correct n and r}
```

```
    writeln('This program computes nCr.');
    writeln;
    repeat
      write('Enter n and r, both integers >= Ø .. ');
      readln(n,r);
    until (n>=Ø) and (r>=Ø);

    {Escape if both n and r are 999}

    if (n=999) and (r=999) then goto 1Ø;

    {Compute nCr by recurrence from 1 to r}

    nCr:=1;    {nCo is always 1}
    for counter:=1 to r do
      nCr:=(n-r+counter)*nCr div counter;

    writeln('Number of combinations is',nCr)

  until false;
1Ø:              {Empty statement}
end.
```

Only a statement can be labelled. This is why in the above example the **label** was placed on an empty statement before **end**. This is because **end** is not a statement—**begin** . . . **end** is a statement but **end** is not. The empty statement is available to use as the target for a **goto**, and is only useful before **end**. Perhaps the originators of Pascal detested **goto** so much that they made this deliberately confusing. The effect of the empty statement is to allow extra semicolons in any statement sequence. It seems as if a semicolon before **end** or **until** is optional, except if there is a label present when it becomes compulsory. The last two lines of the above program could be:

```
  until false;
1Ø:end.
```

Actually the semicolon goes with the labelled empty statement before **end**. Confused? In the next chapter some simple rules are given to help with the semicolon.

Pascal will not permit a program to jump to the inside of any statement from outside. Recall that statements often contain statements. For example a **goto** cannot jump to any of the statements inside a **begin** . . . **end** sequence from either before the **begin** or after the **end**. It can jump from one place to another inside the structure, or it can jump out.

Notice that the **goto** in the $_nC_r$ program escapes downwards towards the end of the program. A **goto** which jumps to an earlier part of a program is always best replaced by a **repeat** . . . **until** structure. When tempted to use **goto**, ask first 'Is there a better way?' Use it as a last resort, and only if it actually improves the clarity of a program compared to the alternatives.

7 Problems

Problem 7.1 Find all the prime factors of a number. If a factor is repeated, you should find it more than once. This problem is best done by reducing the number each time a factor is found, and then starting again.

Problem 7.2 A perfect number is one all of whose factors (prime or otherwise) other then itself add up to itself, for example

$$6 = 1 + 2 + 3$$
$$28 = 1 + 2 + 4 + 7 + 14$$

Euclid spoiled a lot of fun by giving a formula for all the even ones. Find an odd perfect number.

Problem 7.3 Using loops this time, find how many right angled triangles there are with integer sides all of length < 1000.

Problem 7.4 The power series expansions of some common functions are surprisingly efficient, and of some others are surprisingly inefficient. Most can be evaluated using recurrence. Write programs to evaluate:

$$e^x = 1 + x + \frac{x^2}{2} + \frac{x^3}{3!} + \ldots$$

$$\ln(1+x) = x - \frac{x^2}{2} + \frac{x^3}{3} - \frac{x^4}{4} + \ldots$$

$$\sin x = x - \frac{x^3}{3!} + \frac{x^5}{5!} - \frac{x^7}{7!} + \ldots$$

$$\cos x = 1 - \frac{x^2}{2!} + \frac{x^4}{4!} - \frac{x^6}{6!} + \ldots$$

Which of these are efficient and which are inefficient? Do the recurrence relationships give any guidance in estimating the residual errors after n terms and the expected rate of convergence for these series? Would you use any of them if you were asked to write your own algorithms to give answers correct to 6 decimal places?

Eight
About structure

1 Organizing programs

The term *structure* is widely used to describe different aspects of programs and programming. To avoid confusion, I will use *structure* in describing the sequence of events in a program, and refer separately to the *form* of a program as the way that it is laid out. Structured types for representing data are introduced in Chapters 15 to 18.

The structured statements of Pascal are designed to express current ideas about organizing a well structured program. The structured statements are

begin . . . **end**	(the compound statement)
if . . . **then** . . . **else**	
while . . . **do**	
repeat . . . **until**	
for . . . **do**	
case . . . **of**	(introduced in this chapter)
with . . . **do**	(introduced in Chapter 16)

The basic idea behind structured programming is that any program, however complex, should be easily understood by a human who reads it. It is clear that a well structured program does not contain a lot of jumps from here to there. In other words the **goto** is used sparingly if at all. This chapter summarizes the structures as they appear in Pascal, and introduces one new one—the **case** statement.

Flow diagrams have largely fallen from grace as a means of describing programs. If a program reads well, then a diagram of it is hardly necessary. However, flow diagrams are used in this chapter to illustrate the basic structures, to assist those converting to Pascal who may be accustomed to them. Only two symbols are used. The diamond shape is used to represent a *decision* because it can be conveniently left in several directions, while the box is simply a *process*.

The most direct structure is one of sequence. All computer languages obey instructions given in sequence. This could be the action part of a Pascal program:

```
begin
   setitallup;
   dothething;
   closeitdown;
end.
```

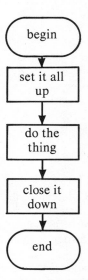

In fact, this is a very likely program. Each line activates a procedure, and making procedures is the subject of the next chapter.

The structure of a program may include various decisions. The simplest of these is the choice of carrying out a process or not. In Pascal this is expressed by the **if** statement:

> **if** *condition* **then** *process*

for example

```
if first>second then
  begin
    save:=first;
    first:=second;
    second:=save
  end
```

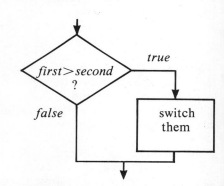

Slightly different is the choice between two alternatives in which the **else** would be used with **if**:

```
if maybe then
  writeln('It is prime')
else
  writeln('It is not prime')
```

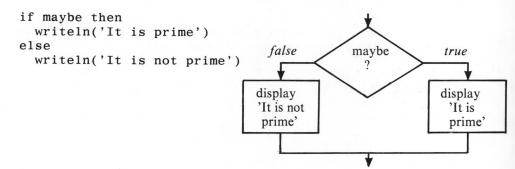

When the choice is among several cases, either a series of **if** statements could be used or the **case** structure, which is introduced in the next section.

In Pascal there are three structures for iteration. The **while** structure decides at the beginning:

```
nshriek:=1;
while n>1 do
   begin
      nshriek:=nshriek*n;
      n:=n−1
   end
```

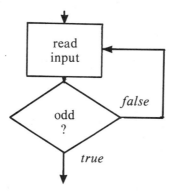

The **repeat** structure decides at the end, and is therefore always done at least once:

```
repeat
   write('Enter an odd number .. ');
   readln(oddone)
until odd(oddone)
```

The **for** statement covers the very common case of counting, and resembles **while** in the sense that it may not be done at all:

```
nCr:=1;
for counter:=1 to r do
   nCr:=(n−r+counter)*nCr div counter
```

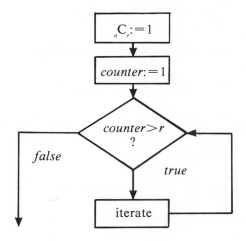

2 The case structure

In the action part of a program, when a choice is to be made between several alternatives, a series of **if** statements could be used:

```
if daynumber=1 then writeln('Sunday');
if daynumber=2 then writeln('Monday');
if daynumber=3 then writeln('Tuesday');
if daynumber=4 then writeln('Wednesday');
if daynumber=5 then writeln('Thursday');
if daynumber=6 then writeln('Friday');
if daynumber=7 then writeln('Saturday')
```

However, Pascal has a **case** structure which would often be preferred:

```
program weekday;
  var daynumber:integer;
  begin
    write('Enter day number .. ');
    readln(daynumber);
    case daynumber of
      1: writeln('Sunday');
      2: writeln('Monday');
      3: writeln('Tuesday');
      4: writeln('Wednesday');
      5: writeln('Thursday');
      6: writeln('Friday');
      7: writeln('Saturday')
    end;
```

The **case** statement can be used to select one of a range of alternative choices in a program. It is best used when the choices are equally likely, at least approximately:

> **case** *expression* **of**
>   *list*: *statement*;
>   *list*: *statement*;
>
>   .
>   .
>   .
>
>   *list*: *statement*
> **end**

The *expression* is of any type that can be ordered. It can be integer or boolean, but not real. It can also be of type char (Chapter 13) or an enumerated or subrange type created by the program (Chapter 15).

When the **case** statement is executed, the *expression* is evaluated, and the value it gives must occur in one of the *list*s. The appropriate *statement* is then taken, but not any of the others. The *statement* could of course be a compound statement.

Each *list* is a list of constants, separated by commas, of the same type as the *expression*. Often this may look like a **goto** label, but it is not the same thing.

The character type can be used in the **case** statement. Characters are introduced in Chapter 13, but here is an example. *Letter* is a character variable, and it is desired to know which of the London telephone directories it belongs in.

```
case letter of
   'a','b','c','d':writeln('A to D');
   'e','f','g','h','i','j','k':writeln('E to K');
   'l','m','n','o','p','q','r':writeln('L to R');
   's','t','u','v','w','x','y','z':writeln('S to Z')
end
```

If one choice is far more likely than the others, it is probably more efficient to pick that off as a special case using an **if** statement first. The **case** structure could then be part of the **else**:

```
if group=0 then writeln('Majority')
else
   case group of
      1:writeln('Minority group 1');
      2:writeln('Minority group 2');
      3:writeln('Minority group 3')
   end
```

In standard Pascal it is wrong for a **case** statement to miss out a value from its *list*s which might occur. If such a value does occur, the program will fail if it conforms to the standard, or it might select none of the cases. This is inconvenient in many applications and some implementations of Pascal allow an **otherwise** structure, which means effectively 'none of the above':

```
case letter of
  'a','b','c','d':writeln('A to D');
  'e','f','g','h','i','j','k':writeln('E to K');
  'l','m','n','o','p','q','r':writeln('L to R');
  's','t','u','v','w','x','y','z':writeln('S to Z');
otherwise:
  writeln('Not a letter, stupid!')
end
```

However if the **otherwise** case is the most likely one, this is inefficient because the computer has to try all the other values first. Again it is often best to pick off the majority case or cases using **if**.

3 All about semicolons

Nothing in Pascal seems to cause as much confusion as the semicolon. Actually at heart it is quite simple. The semicolon is used to separate either declarations or statements when they occur in a sequence. Statement sequences occur in the **begin** . . . **end** and **repeat** . . . **until** structures. A semicolon actually comes before each additional statement in a sequence. If you remember this, and know what a statement is, you cannot go wrong.

Semicolons go before statements or declarations—not after them

Consider a sequence

```
begin
  save:=first;
  first:=second;
  second:=save
end
```

There are semicolons before every additional statement in the sequence. The same thing happens in

```
repeat
  counter:=counter+1;
  if counter=5 then finished:=true;
  writeln('Counting ',counter)
until finished
```

As a consequence, as long as you are not using **goto**:

(i)   You do not need a semicolon before **end** or **until**;

(ii) You must never put a semicolon before **else**.

These are consequences, not rules. Why are there two of them? Because of the null statement which enables a **goto** label to be inserted just before **end** or **until**. A null statement is not a blank or a newline—it is nothing at all. But it is visible because of the semicolon which separates it from the statement before. So while it may look as if a semicolon is optional before **end** or **until**, if it is there it is actually separating a null statement.

Nine
Procedures

1 This is a procedure

The concept of a procedure (or subroutine) exists in many computer languages, but in Pascal it achieves a powerful and general form. Here the basic principles are developed by a series of examples, with the rules summarized later in the chapter. This is a procedure to write a rude message:

```
procedure berude;

  {A procedure to display a rude message}

  begin
    write('This is a very rude message. ');
    writeln('Consider yourself beruded.')
  end;
```

To use the procedure, it must be written into a program as the last declaration before the action part. Then in the action part the procedure is activated simply by writing its name:

```
program rudeness;
  var howrude:integer;

  procedure berude;

    {A procedure to display a rude message}

    begin
      write('This is a very rude message. ');
      writeln('Consider yourself beruded.')
    end;

  {This is the main program}

  begin
    for howrude:=1 to 25 do berude
  end.
```

2 Parameter passing

Most of the time a program will wish to pass information to a procedure, or to obtain information from it. Suppose for the moment that a value is to be passed to a procedure. As an example, you want to display the result of a boolean expression as either YES or NO instead of TRUE or FALSE. This procedure can do it:

```
procedure yesorno(booleanvalue:boolean);

  {Procedure to display boolean value}

  begin
    case booleanvalue of
      true:write('YES');
      false:write('NO')
    end
end;
```

Here the boolean value *booleanvalue* is a formal parameter which is used like a variable within the procedure. To pass it an actual value, bind it into a program as the last declaration:

```
program eoar;

  {Simulate the exclusive or operation}

  var a,b,eor:boolean;
      ina,inb:integer;

  {Put the procedure yesorno here}

  {Main program starts here}

  begin
    repeat
      write('Enter two values, Ø is no .. ');
      readln(ina,inb);
      a:=true;
      if ina=Ø then a:=false;
      b:=true;
      if inb=Ø then b:=false;

      {Echo the given values}

      write('You gave me a = ');
      yesorno(a);
      write(' and b = ');
      yesorno(b);
      writeln;

      {work out and display a EOR b}
```

```
      eor:=(a and not b) or (b and not a);
      write('The exclusive OR of these is ');
      yesorno(eor);
      writeln
   until false
end.
```

In general a parameter list provides the local names of the parameters and their type. These are called the *formal parameters* of the procedure:

```
procedure forexample(i,j:integer;maybe:boolean;b,c,g:real);
```

Note how these occur grouped by type. When the procedure is used the correct number of parameters is given. These must correspond by their type and order with the formal parameter list.

3 Value or name

The example in the previous section passed a value to a procedure. Often you may want a procedure to pass some value back to you. Pascal distinguishes between *value parameters* which carry values into procedures and *variable parameters* which can also carry them back. These methods are often called 'call by value' and 'call by name'.

Value parameters send values to a procedure.

Variable parameters can also carry them back.

In some programming languages, FORTRAN in particular, all subroutine parameters are called by name. It is important in Pascal to appreciate the distinction. Compare these two programs:

```
program value;

   {Demonstrates a value parameter}

   var test:integer;

   procedure cube(number:integer);

      {displays cube of number}

      begin
        number:=number*number*number;
        writeln('The cube is ',number)
      end;

   {Main program}
```

```
begin
  test:=3;
  writeln('The test value is ',test);
  cube(test);
  writeln('Now the test value is ',test)
end.
```

This program calls a procedure by value. The cube of 3, which is 27, is displayed but when the procedure has finished the value of *test* is still 3. If a procedure alters a value parameter, it only alters its own temporary copy. The above program has altered its own local copy called *number*, but it has not changed *test*.

This one is completely different:

```
program name;

  {Demonstrates a variable parameter}

  var test:integer;

  procedure cube(var number:integer);

    {cubes and displays number}

    begin
      number:=number*number*number;
      writeln('The cube is ',number)
    end;

  {Main program}

  begin
    test:=3;
    writeln('The test value is ',test);
    cube(test);
    writeln('Now the test value is ',test)
  end.
```

The **var** in the parameter list in this case specifies that *number* is a variable parameter. When the procedure alters *number*, the variable *test* also changes. This is a very important distinction.

A mixed group of value and variable parameters could be presented as shown in this example:

```
procedure zamp(var a,b:integer;x:real;var booby:boolean)
```

Here *x* is a real value parameter. The others are all variable parameters.

> *Exercise* Write and test a procedure inputter which prompts the user for an integer value between given limits. It persists until a correct integer is entered, which is passed back.

4 Local or global

In passing a value parameter to a procedure, we have seen that a procedure often works with its own private (and temporary) copy of a value. The same idea extends to variables which can be created inside a procedure and are known only within the procedure itself. In fact the index variable of a **for** loop must be one of these local variables.

Example In this program the procedure *ordure* has two variable parameters *x* and *y* passed to it, but it also has a local variable called *t*:

```
program reorder;

  {Global variable declarations}

  var a,b:integer;

  procedure ordure(var x,y:integer);

    {A procedure to order parameters x and y so
        that x<=y. If x=y they are not switched.}

    var t:integer;     {Local to this procedure}

    begin
      writeln('Ordure has   ',x,y);
      if x>y then
        begin
          writeln('Switching');
          t:=x; x:=y; y:=t
        end;
    end;


  {Main program}

  begin
    write('Enter two numbers to put in order .. ');
    readln(a,b);
    ordure(a,b);
    writeln('Now in order',a,b)
  end.
```

The variables *a* and *b* are *global variables* available to all parts of the program. They could have been used in the procedure *ordure* but they were not. The variable *t* is known only inside *ordure*—it could not have been used in the main program. We will see in the next chapter that when we nest procedures the choice is not quite as simple as local or global.

There is a special rule which applies to the variable used to count in a **for** statement. The **for** index has to be a local variable declared in the block that actually uses it. (Furthermore, the **for** index cannot be passed as a **var** parameter to a procedure or function, although it can be passed as a value parameter. Pascal is taking no chances that a **for** index can be altered by a program.) This is correct:

```
program correct;

   var cols:integer;

   procedure stars(nstars:integer);

      {Display a row of n stars}

      var counts:integer;
      begin
        for counts:=1 to nstars do write('*');
        writeln
      end;

   {Main program plots a pyramid}

   begin
     for cols:=1 to 1Ø do stars(2*cols);
     for cols:=9 downto 1 do stars(2*cols)
   end.
```

Notice that *nstars* is a value parameter, and the value passed by the main program is 2*cols. The global variable *cols* can be used as a **for** index in the main program (but not in the procedure even though it is known there). The local variable *counts* can be used as a **for** index in the procedure but not in the main program (where it is unknown anyway).

You will need to know what happens if a global name is redefined as either a parameter or the name of a local variable within a procedure. In either case the new local variable is not the same as the global with the same name. Both of these cases occur in the example which follows.

Example

```
program renames;

   {Demonstrates how a procedure can
      redefine identifiers}

   var i,n:integer;     {Global variables}

   procedure shriek(n:integer);
      var i,nshriek:integer;   {Local variables}
      begin
        nshriek:=1;
```

```
    for i:=1 to n do
      nshriek:=nshriek*i;
    writeln('The factorial of',n:3,' is',nshriek:6);
    end;

  begin
    writeln('Program lists factorials up to a maximum');
    repeat
      write('Enter positive or zero maximum .. ');
      readln(n)
    until n>-1;
    for i:=0 to n do shriek(i)
  end.
```

The main program uses the global variables *i* and *n*. Normally the procedure *shriek* would be able to use both of them also. However in this example they are redefined—*i* is used as a local variable, and *n* is a value parameter. The *i* and *n* used inside the procedure are not the same as the *i* and *n* used by the main program—in fact main program *i* gets used as the value of local *n* when the procedure is used.

Actually it is not a good idea to do this—it only confuses people as you will probably agree. This program does exactly the same thing without changing the meaning of any identifier:

```
program samething;

  var max,index:integer;     {Global variables}

  procedure shriek(n:integer);
    var i,nshriek:integer;   {Local variables}
    begin
      nshriek:=1;
      for i:=1 to n do
        nshriek:=nshriek*i;
      writeln('The factorial of',n:3,' is',nshriek:6);
    end;

  begin
    writeln('Program lists factorials up to a maximum');
    repeat
      write('Enter positive or zero maximum .. ');
      readln(max)
    until max>-1;
    for index:=0 to max do shriek(index)
  end.
```

Exercise Using a similar idea, plot a graph of a sine wave on your terminal using a series of spaces followed by a star to place each value of the sine in the correct column.

5 Recursion

This may come as a surprise, but in Pascal a procedure can call itself. If you want to print the numbers from 1 to 10, why not print 10 after printing the numbers 1 to 9? This one does:

```
program recursive;

   {Demonstrates a procedure calling itself}

   procedure counts(nstart:integer);
     begin
       if nstart>1 then counts(nstart−1);
       writeln(nstart)
     end;

   {Main program}

   begin
     counts(10)
   end.
```

Here the procedure *counts* is given a value parameter *nstart*. It calls itself, passing on *nstart* − 1, and this will go on until the value parameter *nstart* is reduced to one. Now comes the clever bit. The value of *nstart* is written (1), and the end of the procedure is reached, whereupon the procedure returns from its last call where the value of *nstart* was 2, and so on. The first call is the last one to come out. Run this program and it displays the integers from 1 to 10 in that order. To display them backwards, interchange the **if** and *writeln* statements.

Why does it work? Because a new set of local variables and value parameters is created for each 'activation' of the procedure, and these are remembered for that activation until it is completed.

Example Because a **for** variable is always a local variable, this program is a counter counter:

```
program countcount;

   procedure zowie(limit:integer);

   {Government Health Warning : Highly Recursive}

     var i:integer;

     begin
       for i:=1 to limit do zowie(limit−1);
       write(limit:3)
     end;

   begin
     zowie(5)
   end.
```

In the chapters which follow, there are several more examples of recursion. Several recursive functions appear in Chapter 11. A recursive method of sorting information occurs in Chapter 12. You may particularly enjoy the anagram program in Chapter 13.

Exercise If you are trying to convert a decimal number to another base, as in Chapter 3, the digits of the answer come out in the wrong order. If, however, you find the digits by a recursive procedure, you can make them come out either forwards or backwards. Do it.

6 Recursion using several procedures—mutual recursion

Example Here is another way to make a pyramid:

```
program cheopcheop;

   {Somewhat recursive pyramid builder}

   procedure stellar(nstars:integer);
     begin
       if nstars>1 then stellar(nstars-1);
       write('*')
     end;

   procedure rise(high:integer);
     begin
       if high>1 then rise(high-1);
       stellar(2*high);
       writeln
     end;

   procedure fall(high:integer);
     begin
       stellar(2*high);
       writeln;
       if high>1 then fall(high-1)
     end;

   procedure pyramid(height:integer);
     begin
       rise(height);
       fall(height-1);
     end;

   {Main program}

   begin
     pyramid(1Ø)
   end.
```

The example above is the first instance of a program containing several procedures which variously call each other (and themselves). In Pascal there is a basic rule concerning procedures, which is that they must be defined before the line of program which calls them. This is part of the general rule that an identifier is declared before it is used. (A procedure name is an identifier; **procedure** is a declaration.)

Almost always a program can obey this rule. Only in special circumstances—a recursion in which procedures call each other in a circle—is this impossible. This is called *mutual recursion,* and to achieve it a *forward* directive is used. The parameters are defined with the *forward* directive, and the actual body of the procedure which comes later contains the declarations and actions.

Example This program contains *forward* directives. It carries on one side of a most interesting conversation:

```
program courting;

  {Demonstrates a forward directive}

  procedure sayJohn(times:integer);
    forward;

  procedure sayNo(times:integer);
    var i:integer;
    begin
      for i:=1 to times do sayJohn(times-1);
      for i:=1 to times do write('No. ');
      writeln

    end;

  procedure sayJohn;
    var i:integer;
    begin
      for i:=1 to times do sayNo(times-1);
      for i:=1 to times do write('John! ');
      writeln
    end;

  {Main program}

  begin
    sayJohn(4)
  end.
```

If a program has been properly defined, *forward* directives are not necessary except in these special recursive circumstances.

Exercise Can you do the pyramid in fewer procedures—fully recursive and no loops!

7 Procedure names as parameters

Procedure parameters can be values, variables or the names of other procedures or functions. Handled with care this is sometimes useful (but not often). In the **procedure** declaration a parameter can appear which represents another **procedure** declaration. For example the procedure

```
procedure plotcos(procedure show (cc:integer));
```

could have inside it a reference to the procedure *show*:

```
show(round(value)+offset)
```

Plotcos does not find out the real name of procedure *show* until it is passed the name of an actual procedure, for example

```
plotcos(plunkit)
```

This will work if:

1) *Plunkit* is the name of an actual procedure.

2) The parameters of the actual *plunkit* correspond exactly with those stated for procedure *show*. They must match according to whether they are value, variable or procedure parameters, and according to their type, and they must be in the correct order.

3) The procedure *plunkit* must be a declaration available to both the main program and the procedure *plotcos*. In effect this means they must be part of the same block, as explained in the next chapter. This also rules out the use of standard procedures (like *writeln*) and functions (like *sin*) as arguments—although some implementations will allow this.

With the name of a function as a parameter, the type is also given. An example using functions is given in Chapter 11.

> *Example* Two procedures are available for representing a point on a graph, both declared in this program. To plot a graph of a cosine the user has a choice of these in calling the procedure *plotcos*. In the program, both are done:
>
> ```
> program cosplot;
>
>     {Demonstrates passing of a procedure name}
>
>     procedure plunkit(column:integer);
>
>        {Plots a star at column column}
>
>        var col:integer;
>        begin
>          for col:=column downto 2 do write(' ');
>          writeln('*')
>        end;
> ```

```
procedure shadit(column:integer);

  {Plots a solid bar to column column}

  var col:integer;
  begin
    for col:=column downto 1 do write('*');
    writeln
  end;

procedure plotcos(procedure show(cc:integer));

  {Plots a 60 column wide graph between columns
   10 and 70 of cos(x) using the procedure show}

  const nsteps=16;
        width=60;
        offset=10;
        xmin=0.0;
        xmax=6.2831853;

  var look:integer;
      x,step:real;
      value,scale:real;

  begin
    scale:=width/2;
    step:=(xmax-xmin)/nsteps;
    for look:=0 to nsteps do              {Main program}
      begin
        x:=xmin+step*look;                begin
        value:=(cos(x)+1)*scale;            plotcos(plunkit);
        show(round(value)+offset)           plotcos(shadit);
      end                                   plotcos(plunkit)
  end;                                    end.
```

8 Rules about procedures

In general, the final declaration in any declaration part of a Pascal program can be one or more procedures or functions. The **procedure** declaration is

> **procedure** *name(formal parameters)*;
> *declarations*;
> *compound statement*;

The *formal parameters* identify names which will be used by the procedure as if they were variables known inside the procedure (or the names of procedures and functions in the rare case of procedure or function parameters). A variable parameter carries its value back when the procedure is finished, as was discussed in Section 3 of this chapter.

Value parameters are specified as

> *name, name, name*: *type name*; *name, name*: *type name* . . .

Variable parameters have in addition the keyword **var**:

> **var** *name*: *type name*; **var** *name, name*: *type name* . . .

The declarations that appear inside a procedure apply to that procedure alone. They are in the usual order: **label**; **const**; **type**; **var**; **procedure**s or **function**s.

The compound statement defines the actions taken by the procedure—like all compound statements it begins with **begin** and ends with **end**. The **end** marks the end of what is effectively the declaration of a procedure. What follows will either be another procedure or function (Chapter 11), or the action part of the block containing the procedure. In either case it will be separated by a semicolon.

You will note that I have referred to the 'block' containing the procedure. All the examples in this chapter have been of main programs containing a number of procedures, and all of them can call each other. Things get a bit more complex when a procedure contains another procedure. The next chapter describes the form of Pascal programs in general.

There are two other forms of the procedure:

(i)   With a *forward* or *external* directive. *External* specifies that a procedure is not found in this Pascal program but is in some library. The arrangements for binding external procedures into programs vary widely between computers:

> **procedure** *name*(*parameters*);
>   *external*;

The *forward* directive is not actually necessary unless a program features mutual recursion as was discussed in Section 5 of this chapter. *Forward* means that the declarations and action part come later:

> **procedure** *name*(*parameters*);
>   *forward*;

With both *forward* and *external* the full formal parameter list for the procedure is required.

(ii) Without the parameters given, the procedure is to be the actual definition of a procedure earlier directed *forward*.

Like any other declaration a **procedure** must be defined before it is referred to. This is why the *forward* and *external* directives are required. This simple rule has important implications about the form of Pascal programs, which is the subject of the next chapter.

When you use a procedure, the actual parameters are passed to the procedure:

> *name*(*actual parameters*)

The actual parameters must agree with the formal parameters in the procedure declaration. There must be the same number, in the same order, and of a correct type. Remember if you want results to be passed back to use variable parameters. Many examples of procedures occur in the rest of this text.

9 Problems

Problem 9.1 Write a procedure *torectangular* which converts its two real parameters from polar form to rectangular form. If (r, θ) is a polar coordinate, then the rectangular one (x, y) is

$$x = r \cos \theta$$
$$y = r \sin \theta$$

Then write a procedure *topolar* which does the opposite.

Problem 9.2 The vector in Fig. 9.1 has its tail at the origin and its head in one of the eight positions numbered from 1 to 8. The coordinates of the head can be any pair of the values -1, 0 or 1 except (0,0). Write a procedure *swingit* which moves given integer coordinates of the head by n positions clockwise, where n is the third parameter, and could be positive, zero or negative. For example,

```
swingit(1,1,  3)
```

should swing it from position 1 to position 6 in Fig. 9.1.

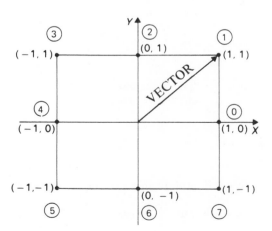

Fig. 9.1. A procedure is required to swing the tip of the vector.

Problem 9.3 Write a procedure to find and display all the prime factors of a number without any **for**, **while** or **repeat** loops, i.e. use only recursion. Make it write the primes in order from largest to smallest. Then make it display from smallest to largest.

Problem 9.4 The Towers of Hanoi is an entertainment used to illustrate the process of recursion. There are three poles. On one sits a tower of n rings, which are all different sizes arranged from largest at the base to smallest at the top, Fig. 9.2. Write a program which shows all the steps in moving the tower to another pole one ring at a time without ever placing a larger ring on top of a smaller one. Try to do it without looking it up anywhere.

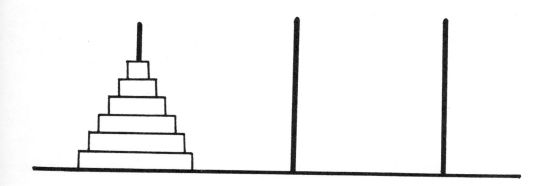

Fig. 9.2. The Towers of Hanoi.

Ten
About form

1 Programs with procedures

A program has grammar, structure and form. The grammar, or *syntax*, of a program specifies the rules of construction of statements. The structure is the way a programmer puts the grammar together to achieve the objectives of the program. The form is the shape the program must take as it is presented to the computer. The meaning of a program is defined by the *semantics* of Pascal.

Every program in Pascal consists of a *heading* followed by a *block*:

> *heading* {*one* **program** *statement*};
>
> | *declarations*; |
> | *action* {*one compound statement*}. |

In Pascal, every name or identifier must be defined before it is used. This dictates the basic form as shown above, and it also dictates how procedures and functions fit in. Expanding the block to give details of the declarations gives:

> *heading* {*one* **program** *statement*};
>
> | *declarations* **label**; |
> | **const**; |
> | **type**; |
> | **var**; |
> | **procedures** *or* **functions**; |
> | *action* {*one compound statement*}. |

The procedures or functions have access to all the identifiers defined by the declarations shown, as does the action part which is traditionally called the *main program*. These identifiers are said to be *global* in scope because they are available to all parts of the program.

Now add a procedure. A procedure has a heading which is the **procedure** declaration and which is followed by a block of exactly the same form as the main block which contains it.

You can see in this the beginning of an indentation scheme in which each inner block is indented compared to the block that contains it. This is not a requirement—but it makes programs easier to understand because the form becomes more visible.

heading {*one* **program** *statement*};

> *declarations*;
> *heading* {**procedure** *declarations*};
>
> > *declarations*;
> > *action* {*one compound statement*};
>
> *action* {*one compound statement*}.

With one block containing another, it is important to distinguish the scope of names declared in the main block and the procedure block. The global declarations are available everywhere, including the procedure. By contrast, the names declared within the procedure are not available to the outer or containing block. The general rule is:

> *Inner blocks know outer declarations.*

> *Outer blocks do not know inner declarations.*

2 Procedures within procedures

Now we complicate the issue by having procedures (or functions) within procedures (or functions). The general rules still apply. Although programs can be much more complex, all the basic principles are evident in this one:

program *outer*;

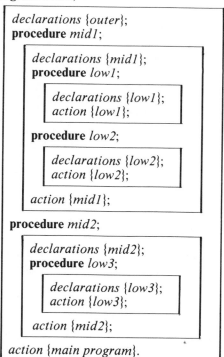

> *declarations* {*outer*};
> **procedure** *mid1*;
>
> > *declarations* {*mid1*};
> > **procedure** *low1*;
> >
> > > *declarations* {*low1*};
> > > *action* {*low1*};
> >
> > **procedure** *low2*;
> >
> > > *declarations* {*low2*};
> > > *action* {*low2*};
> >
> > *action* {*mid1*};
>
> **procedure** *mid2*;
>
> > *declarations* {*mid2*};
> > **procedure** *low3*;
> >
> > > *declarations* {*low3*};
> > > *action* {*low3*};
> >
> > *action* {*mid2*};
>
> *action* {*main program*}.

The action part of the main program outer has access to its own declarations only. This means that it can use labels, constants, types or variables only from the outer declarations. It can also use only the procedures *mid1* and *mid2*.

The procedure *mid1* has access to the outer global declarations and its own declarations. It can use labels, constants, types and variables from {*outer*} or {*mid1*} declarations. It can call procedures *low1* or *low2*, itself (if recursive), or *mid2* with a *forward* declaration. Looking at mid1 negatively, it does not have access to declarations in *mid2* and it cannot use the procedure *low3*.

Similarly *mid2* can use its own declarations and global ones, and it can call procedures *low3*, *mid2* (recursively) or *mid1*. It cannot make use of declarations inside *mid1*, which means that it cannot call *low1* or *low2*.

Looking at the low procedures, the available and unavailable items can be tabulated:

Name	Declarations available	Declarations not available
low1	*outer*	*mid2*
	mid1	*low2*
	low1	*low3*
low2	*outer*	*mid2*
	mid1	*low1*
	low2	*low3*
low3	*outer*	*mid1*
	mid2	*low1*
	low3	*low2*

Name	Procedures available	Procedures not available
low1	*low1* (recursive)	*mid2*
	mid1 (recursive)	*low3*
	low2 (forward)	
low2	*low2* (recursive)	*mid2*
	mid1 (recursive)	*low3*
	low1	
low3	*low3* (recursive)	*mid1*
	mid2 (recursive)	*low1*
		low2

3 Sermon on the scope

It is generally agreed that Pascal encourages programmers to write well structured programs, meaning that the actions taken by a program can be expressed in a straightforward and easy to understand manner. There is, of course, no way of preventing foul programs from being written by a determined person.

The rule that an identifier must be declared before it is used dictates the form of a Pascal program. This feature of Pascal enables it to ensure that identifiers are used consistently and correctly. This prevents common programming errors which occur in other languages from occurring in Pascal, at least most of the time. In particular, Pascal is unlikely to allow you to misspell or mistype the name of an identifier (when that kind of error does occur it is all the more agonizing because of its rarity in Pascal).

The block form of Pascal does present a few problems, however. It can be difficult to see the scope of a particular identifier, and programmers can set traps for themselves. Pascal's greatest weakness probably lies in this aspect of the scoping of variables. Here I try to give some guidelines to help you avoid these problems.

In Pascal, labels and the names of types, constants, variables and procedures or functions are declared before they are used. Because of the block form of programs, there is often a choice of where to declare a particular identifier. The problems arise when a programmer revisits a program (possibly written by someone else) to make some changes. If a variable, for example, is not a local one then it is often very difficult to know what use is being made of it by other parts of the program. A simple change to one procedure could bring the whole program to a halt!

Recommendation 1: Use local names wherever possible.

If there is no good reason to widen their scope, then labels and identifiers may as well be local to the procedures or functions which use them. The variables which control **for** loops have to be local anyway. I know of two good reasons in particular circumstances when local variables cannot be used:

(i)   A quantity may be shared—obvious.

(ii) You may want the value of a variable to be remembered next time around. Pascal creates its variables from scratch each time a procedure or function is used. One day you will trip up on this!

There is, incidentally, no reason why the same local name should not be used in lots of different procedures.

Recommendation 2: If it is not local then make it global.

If you do this, then a programmer can locate the definition of an identifier more easily, by looking at the declarations in the same block and the global declarations. They will be grateful! But don't trust others to do the same. To be sure of finding the declaration of a label or identifier you have to search outwards through all the containing blocks to find the nearest definition. Then you know that the scope of the declaration is the nearest containing block in which you find it.

Recommendation 3: Never redefine an identifier or label.

Pascal will allow the meaning of an identifier to be changed either as a formal parameter of a procedure or function or in a declaration. Either way if the identifier occurred in a containing block, its meaning changes throughout the inner block. It is actually a new name with a new scope. Programmers can inflict dreadful injuries in this way. A small example was given in the previous chapter—program *renames*.

```
program renames;

  {Demonstrates how a procedure can
    redefine identifiers}

  var i,n:integer;    {Global variables}

  procedure shriek(n:integer);
    var i,nshriek:integer;  {Local variables}
    begin
      nshriek:=1;
      for i:=1 to n do
        nshriek:=nshriek*i;
      writeln('The factorial of',n:3,' is',nshriek:6);
    end;

  begin
    writeln('Program lists factorials up to a maximum');
    repeat
      write('Enter positive or zero maximum .. ');
      readln(n)
    until n>-1;
    for i:=0 to n do shriek(i)
  end.
```

If you do, it is the nearest definition in a containing block that applies. Look up through the containing blocks to find it.

In recommendation 1 I said there was nothing wrong with using the same local name in lots of places. Do not confuse these two recommendations.

In conclusion, my children, I recognize that I am sermonizing about concepts which cannot be demonstrated well without massive programs. Perhaps you will have to go out into the real world and get yourselves thoroughly enmeshed in these problems before you can appreciate the good advice you have been given. That is life.

Eleven

Functions

1 This is a function

A function is like a procedure except that it is used as part of an expression rather than on its own. This means that a function has a type and produces a result of that type. The type of a function is specified in the **function** heading, which is otherwise similar to a **procedure** heading. The types available are the real type or any ordered type which includes integer, boolean, character (Chapter 13) and subrange or enumerated types that you may define yourself (Chapter 15). You can also have a function which gives a result which is a pointer (Chapter 18). A value must be assigned to the function name within the action part of the function. The function name is not regarded by the function as a local variable.

Example This program displays the truth table of the boolean *nand* function (meaning '**not and**'). Observe the type of the function at the end of its heading, and the assignment of a value to its name (*nand*) within it:

```
program truthtable;
  {Display truth table of NAND function}
  var a,b:boolean;

  function nand(one,two:boolean):boolean;
    {Logical function for not and}
    begin
      nand:=not(one and two)
    end;

{Main Program}

begin
  writeln('    a      b    a NAND b');
  writeln;
  for a:=false to true do
    for b:=false to true do
      begin
        writeln(a:7,b:7,nand(a,b):7)
      end;
end.
```

Exercise Write a boolean **function** *prime(number:integer):boolean* which tells you if *number* is prime.

2 Some real functions

There are many real functions that you might wish to define. Perhaps because Pascal lacks an operator to raise a number to a power, we might begin with this. Not all numbers can be raised to all powers. In particular, fractional powers of negative numbers have no meaning as real numbers (they produce a complex result which does not occur in Pascal). This function provides

$$base^{power}$$

for positive *base*s and an error message with result 0.0 for negative *base*s. Here it is with a minimal test program:

```
program trypow;

  var b,p:real;

  {Test real function pow}

  function pow(base,power:real):real;

    {Raise base to the power but stay
     out of trouble if base is negative}

    var zow:real;

    begin
      if base<=∅.∅ then
        begin
          pow:=∅.∅;
          writeln('Illegal base in fuction pow = ',base)
        end
      else
        pow:=exp(power*ln(base))
    end;

{Main program}        begin
                        write('Enter base and power .. ');
                        readln(b,p);
                        writeln(b,p,pow(b,p))
                      end.
```

Example A remainder function for real numbers might be very useful. How, for example, do you compute the phase of the moon at a particular time? Real **div** is easy to make into a function:

```
function rdiv(num,denom:real):real;
  begin
    rdiv:=trunc(num/denom)
  end;
```

In *rdiv* we are looking for the whole number of times *denom* goes into *num*. The fraction left over would be *rmod*:

```
function rmod(num,denom:real):real;
   begin
      rmod:=num−denom*rdiv(num,denom)
   end;
```

Example The power series for sin x converges very rapidly if x is small enough:

$$\sin x = x - \frac{x^3}{3!} + \frac{x^5}{5!} - \dots$$

We probably know by now that it is foolish to work out factorials explicitly. There is a recurrence in this series. If the term which uses the power x_n is called t_n, then

$$t_1 = x$$

and

$$t_n = \frac{-x^2\, t_{n-2}}{n(n-1)} \qquad \text{for } n = 3, 5, 7, \dots$$

To make x small so that not too many terms are needed, it is reduced to the range -2π to 2π—an important use of the *rmod* function:

```
function sinex(theta:real):real;

   {Evaluate sin(theta) by power series}

   const  twopie=6.2831853;
   var    number:integer;
          term,sum:real;

   begin

      {First reduce theta}

      theta:=rmod(theta,twopie);
      writeln;
      writeln('The reduced angle is ',theta:1Ø:6);
      writeln;

      {Now do the sum, tracing its progress}

      number:=1;
      term:=theta;
      sum:=term;
      writeln('Term no.     Sum         Term');
      writeln(number:3,sum:14:6,term:1Ø:6);
      while abs(term)>1.Øe−5 do
```

```
        begin
          number:=number+2;
          term:=-term*sqr(theta)/(number*(number-1));
          sum:=sum+term;
          writeln(number:3,sum:14:6,term:10:6)
        end;
      sinex:=sum
    end;
```

Exercise The sin x series is more efficient if the angle used is 0 to $\pi/2$ only—with a bit of trigonometry applied to get the right result. Try this and compare it to the above program—that is why it tabulates its results nicely. Then do cos x.

3 Some integer functions

Not surprisingly, there are many uses for integer functions, and two examples are given here.

Example It is easy to make a function to compute $_nC_r$. As we know from Chapter 7 and again from Chapter 9, to avoid problems with huge factorials and also to be more efficient, this recurrence is used:

$$_nC_r = \frac{n-r+1}{r} \cdot {_nC_{r-1}}$$

```
function combs(n,r:integer):integer;

  {nCr function using recurrence}

  var index,result:integer;
  begin
    result:=1;                {nCo is always 1}
    for index:=1 to r do
      result:=(n-r+index)*result div index;
    combs:=result
  end;
```

The function could just as easily be recursive:

```
function recombs(n,r:integer):integer;

  {nCr function using recursive recurrence}

  var result:integer;
  begin
    if r>0 then result:=(n-r+1)*recombs(n,r-1) div r
      else result:=1;
    recombs:=result
  end;
```

Example In a variety of applications ranging from games to mathematical models, random numbers are useful. Computers can very easily produce a series of numbers which appear to be random, although the theory behind it is quite complex. It is often done by multiplying two large numbers together, perhaps even producing a result which is out of range for the computer, and then looking at the remainder of the product with some chosen divisor. Here a multiplier which is always the same is used, to magnify a previous random number whose remainder modulo *maxint* is then scaled to a desired range—remember *maxint*, the largest integer available for which *maxint* and −*maxint* both exist. In my choice of multiplier I have made the assumption that *maxint* is probably 32767. If *maxint* is different on your computer, change the constant *mplyer* to the largest power of 5 which is less than maxint.

It is tested by simulating the throw of two dice, in which the sum of two random numbers in the range 1 to 6 is used. You can enjoy yourself exploring the number of throws taken to produce a 12. The probability of that should be 1 in 36. Do the results you actually get suggest that this is a good or a bad random number generator?

```
program gambler;

   {Test the random number generator by
    throwing dice until a 12 is reached}

   var bignum:integer;   {Global needed by generator}
       thrown:integer;
       countsthem:integer;

   function ran(range:integer):integer;

      {A function to generate a pseudorandom
       integer in the range 1 to range

       The global variable bignum is required
       and must be initialized to an odd value}

      const mplyer=15625;

      begin
        {Get next huge number}
        bignum:=bignum*mplyer mod maxint;
        {Keep them positive}
        if bignum<0 then bignum:=bignum+maxint;
        {And keep them odd}
        if not odd(bignum) then bignum:=bignum+1;
        {Finally the result}
        ran:=trunc(1+range*(bignum/maxint))
      end;

   {Main to throw dice}

   begin
     writeln('This program test random numbers');
```

```
writeln;
repeat
  write('Please enter an odd seed .. ');
  readln(bignum)
until odd(bignum);
countsthem:=∅;
repeat
  thrown:=ran(6)+ran(6);
  writeln('Next throw is ',thrown:3);
  countsthem:=countsthem+1;
until thrown=12;
writeln('It took ',countsthem:4,' throws')
end.
```

Exercise The random number function will always produce a sequence which repeats eventually, but the repetition length is different for different seeds. Write a program to find the repetition length, and use it to find the longest nonrepeating sequence. Also see if you can get rid of the check for even numbers. Then rewrite the random number function to produce a customized generator for your computer.

4 Homage to Pascal (the person, not the language)

Blaise Pascal's name is associated in the mind of every numerate person with the triangular arrangement of binomial coefficients which is called Pascal's triangle:

$$_0C_0$$

$$_1C_0 \quad _1C_1$$

$$_2C_0 \quad _2C_1 \quad _2C_2$$

$$_3C_0 \quad _3C_1 \quad _3C_2 \quad _3C_3 \qquad \text{and so on}$$

There are three recurrences that are of interest here. Best known is that

$$_nC_r = {}_{n-1}C_{r-1} + {}_{n-1}C_r$$

which tells us that each number in the triangle is the sum of the two above it—and so the triangle can be written down very quickly. Less well known is the recurrence we have used to compute $_nC_r$:

$$_nC_r = \frac{n-r+1}{r} \, {}_nC_{r-1}$$

In calculating $_nC_r$ this works along a row of the triangle—so we will use it for displaying a row.

The procedure *triangle* will display the rows of Pascal's triangle by calling itself recursively. A 72 column display is assumed, which is usually safe. Row n is started in column $66-2*n$, and each result is allocated 4 spaces which is adequate for any *n* up to 12—hence the limit of 12 rows. The procedures *tab* and *triangle* and the function *term* are all recursive. *Term* is almost the same as the function *recombs* in the previous section—except that it prints each value it finds and furthermore we throw away the result! You may agree that *term* is like a cross between a procedure and a function:

```
program blazingtriangles;

    {Homage to Mel Pascal or do I mean Blaise Brooks?}

    const maxrows=12;
    var lastrow:integer;

    procedure tabit(col:integer);

      {Move to column col — unnecessary use of recursion}

      begin
        write(' ');
        if col>1 then tabit(col-1)
      end;

    function terms(n,r:integer):integer;

      {Display a row of Mel's triangle
          — recursive recurrence}

      var result:integer;
      begin
        if r>Ø then result:=(n-r+1)*terms(n,r-1) div r
          else result:=1;
        terms:=result;
        write(result:4)
      end;

    procedure triangle(rows:integer);

      {Make Mel's triangle recursively}

      begin
        if rows>Ø then triangle(rows-1);
        writeln;
        tabit(36-2*rows);
        rows:=terms(rows,rows)
      end;

  {Main program}

  begin

    {Obtain the size of the triangle}
```

```
      writeln;
      writeln('This program displays Mel''s triangle');
      writeln;
      writeln('Pascal');
      writeln('   = Blaising triangles');
      writeln('     = Mel Brooks - Get it?');
      writeln;
      repeat
        write('Enter number of rows integer <='
           ,maxrows:4,' .. ');
        readln(lastrow);
      until lastrow<=maxrows;
      triangle(lastrow)
    end.
```

Exercise Can you do this using the other recurrence?

$$_nC_r = {}_{n-1}C_{r-1} + {}_{n-1}C_r$$

5 Passing function names

This is done in the same way as for procedures. Its usefulness is limited, particularly because the names passed have to be known to both the calling and receiving statements. This is so that Pascal can, as always, look after you. It implies that all the identifiers are declared in **procedure** or **function** headings at the same level and in the same block as both the action which passes the parameter and the heading which receives it. Here is a model of how it is done, in which the action part has a choice of styles (*shadit* or *plunkit*) and functions (*sinx* or *cosx*) in calling a graph plotting procedure:

```
program graffer;

    {Demonstrates passing of a function name}

    const pie=3.14159265;

    procedure plunkit(column:integer);

      {Plots a star at column column}

      {Defined in Chapter 9}

      procedure shadit(column:integer);

        {Plots a solid bar to column column}

        {Defined in Chapter 9}

    function sinx(x:real):real;
      begin
        sinx:=sin(x)
      end;
```

```
function cosx(x:real):real;
  begin
    cosx:=cos(x)
  end;

procedure plotagraph(procedure show(cc:integer);
                function func(aa:real):real;
                xmin,xmax:real;nsteps:integer);

  {Plots a 6Ø column wide graph between columns 1Ø
     and 7Ø of the function func using the procedure
     show, between xmin and xmax taking nsteps steps}

  var look:integer;
      x,step:real;
      value,ymin,ymax,scale:real;
  begin
    ymin:=Ø; ymax:=Ø;
    step:=(xmax-xmin)/nsteps;
    for look:=Ø to nsteps do
      begin
        x:=xmin+step*look;
        value:=func(x);
        if value>ymax then ymax:=value
        else if value<ymin then ymin:=value
      end;
    scale:=6Ø/(ymax-ymin);
    for look:=Ø to nsteps do
      begin
        x:=xmin+step*look;
        value:=(func(x)-ymin)*scale;
        show(round(value)+1Ø)
      end
  end;

{Main program}

begin
  plotagraph(shadit,sinx,Ø.Ø,2*pie,16)
end.
```

6 Problems

Problem 11.1 This is an interesting little formula which gives you twice the area of a triangle whose vertices have the coordinates (a,b), (c,d) and (e,f), as shown in Fig. 11.1. The area has a sign which is positive if the order of the coordinates is clockwise, negative if anticlockwise.

$$twicearea = d(e - a) + b(c - e) + f(a - c)$$

Write a real function to find the area of a triangle. Now look at Problem 11.2.

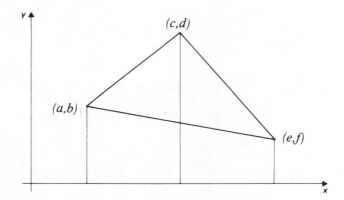

Fig. 11.1. The area of a triangle can be calculated from the co-ordinates of its vertices.

Problem 11.2 You can use the triangle area formula from Problem 11.1 to discover other interesting things, although they require some thought. They work best with integer coordinates, so stick to those in this problem.

(i)   Write a boolean function to tell you if a point (x,y) lies on a line passing through (a,b) and (c,d).

(ii)   Write a boolean function to tell you if a line joining (a,b) to (c,d) intersects the line joining (e,f) to (g,h) between the endpoints, as in Fig. 11.2. Touching counts as intersection.

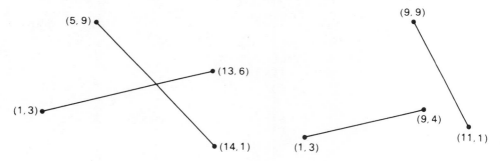

(a) Line segments which intersect.   *(b) Line segments which do not intersect.*

Fig.11.2. Illustrating Problem 11.2 in which line segments are specified by their end co-ordinates.

Problem 11.3 If you take the sum of 12 successive random numbers which lie between 0 and 1, you obtain a value whose probability is an approximation to the Gaussian distribution with mean 6 and variance 1. Make a real function to provide Gaussian random values with zero mean and variance 1. Can you generalize this to any mean μ and variance σ^2?

Problem 11.4 Write integer functions to find the greatest common factor (GCF) and the least common multiple (LCM) of two numbers. There is scope for recursion here.

Twelve
Arrays of one dimension

1 Arrays and indexing

Until now, real and integer variables have been used to represent one value each. There are many circumstances in which a program has to deal with a list of values represented by a single identifier. In Pascal a variable can be an array, simply by declaring it as something like:

```
var iray:array[1..10] of integer;
```

after which the identifier *iray* represents an integer array with integer indices which can vary from 1 to 10. The description

```
array[1..10] of integer
```

describes the type of *iray*. Therefore *iray* is not of type *integer*, it is an array of integers. Each member of the array is of type *integer*. An array is one of the structured types of Pascal.

A member of the array can be accessed in the action part of a program by referring to it with the correct type of index in the declared range, as in the example which follows.

Example In this program you are asked to enter 10 integer values which are placed in the array *iray*. The largest value is then found and displayed:

```
program biggest;

    {Read in an integer array and search
       it for the largest value}

    var iray:array[1..10] of integer;
        index,bigone,where:integer;

    begin

      {Get the array of values}

      writeln('Enter 10 integers for the array');
      for index:=1 to 10 do read(iray[index]);

      {Find the largest value}

      bigone:=iray[1];
      where:=1;
```

```
      for index:=2 to 10 do
        begin
          if bigone<iray[index] then
            begin
              bigone:=iray[index];
              where:=index
            end
        end;
      writeln('The Largest is',bigone:4,' at
        index',where:3)
    end.
```

To read the values into the array, they are obtained one at a time using indices as shown. The *read* and *write* procedures when used with your keyboard and display can only deal with individual values which are *real*, or *integer*, or *char*. (*Write* can also deal with *boolean* values or character strings.) Therefore an indexed arrangement like the one above must be used. This is not the case, however, when dealing with files of the appropriate type, as will be outlined in Chapter 17.

The index of an array is written in square brackets. In some languages round brackets are used for this purpose, which causes confusion with function and procedure or subroutine parameters. In Pascal both you and the language are spared this confusion.

In general, you declare an array variable as

> **var** *identifier*: **array**[*min .. max*] **of** *type*

where

identifier	is the name of the array
min	is a constant which gives the minimum value of the index
max	is a constant which gives the maximum value of the index
type	is the type of values held in the array

The type of *min* and *max* is also important. Usually indices are integers, but in general an index can be of any ordered type, meaning *integer*, *boolean*, *char* as described in Chapter 13, or your own ordered type as introduced in Chapter 15. *Min* and *max* must be constants, both of the same type as the index which will be used with the array, and *max* must occur later in order than *min*.

A reference to an array is made with an index in square brackets. The index must be an expression of the correct type whose value lies in the range from *min* to *max* (including *min* and *max*).

> *Example* Now we can start to get serious about indexing. Here, *ray2* is *ray1* with top and bottom halves interchanged:

```
program swaphalves;

  {Starting to get serious about indexing}
```

```
type swaparray=array[1..8] of integer;

var ray1,ray2:swaparray;
    index:integer;

begin
  for index:=1 to 8 do ray1[index]:=index;

  {Ray2 will be ray1 with halves interchanged}

  for index:=1 to 4 do
    begin
      ray2[index]:=ray1[index+4];
      ray2[index+4]:=ray1[index]
    end;

  {Show before and after}

  writeln('Before:');
  for index:=1 to 8 do write(ray1[index]);
  writeln;
  writeln('After:');
  for index:=1 to 8 do write(ray2[index])
end.
```

*Exercise*Write a program which will accept an array of values and then reverse their order within the array.

2 Assignment of arrays—the type declaration

In an assignment statement in Pascal, a variable can be assigned a value. So why will the assignment of *ray1* to *ray2* in this program not work?

```
program testing;

{Can arrays defined this way be assigned?}

const max=10;

var ray1:array[1..max] of integer;
    ray2:array[1..max] of integer;
    index:integer;

begin
  for index:=1 to max do ray1[index]:=index;
  ray2:=ray1;
  for index:=1 to max do write(ray2[index])
end.
```

The answer is that, although the types of *ray1* and *ray2* are the same, *ray1* and *ray2* are not of
the same *type* if you see the rather fine distinction. To make them the same type, we have to
give the type a name in a **type** declaration, as in this version, which will work:

```
program typing;

   {Arrays defined this way can be assigned!}

   const max=10;

   type testarray=array[1..max] of integer;

   var ray1,ray2:testarray;
       index:integer;

   begin
     for index:=1 to max do ray1[index]:=index;
     ray2:=ray1;
     for index:=1 to max do write(ray2[index])
   end.
```

This is the first time we have used the **type** declaration, which goes between the **const** and **var**
declarations in a Pascal block. The **type** declaration is

$$\textbf{type } typename = type;$$

In order to assign one array to another in a single assignment statement, they must be of the
same type which means that in their **var** declarations they must use the same *typename*.

Because of this they will be exactly the same length. If you want to assign fragments, or use
arrays of different lengths, then the indices will have to be written out in loops.

3 Arrays as procedure or function parameters

There are two ways of passing arrays as parameters in standard Pascal. The one described in
this section is common to all versions of Pascal. It uses a type identifier for the arrays and
does not allow any flexibility in the array size. At the end of this chapter *conformant array
parameters* are described which allow some flexibility in passing arrays of different sizes to
procedures. In both cases, an entire array is passed as a parameter. There is no way of passing
a fragment of an array.

To pass an array by the first method, you have to declare a *type name* for it in a **type**
declaration. In the parameter list of the procedure or function the type has to be given by the
type name.

> *Example* This program uses a procedure to find the largest value in an array. The
> type identifier *demoray* is used to describe the arrays.

```pascal
program findmax;

  {Demonstrate array as parameter}

  type demoray=array[1..4] of integer;

  var   one,two:demoray;
        max,index:integer;

  procedure getaray(var gotray:demoray);

    {Get an array from keyboard}

    var i:integer;

    begin
      writeln('Enter 4 values for an array');
      for i:=1 to 4 do read(gotray[i]);
      writeln
    end;

  procedure getmax(scanray:demoray;
    var value,position:integer);

    {Scan the scanray to find the maximum value
      'value' and its position 'position'}

    var i:integer;

    begin
      value:=scanray[1];
      position:=1;
      for i:=2 to 4 do
        if scanray[i]>value then
          begin
            value:=scanray[i];
            position:=i
          end;
    end;

{Main program}

begin
  writeln('Find the maximum value in each of two arrays');
  getaray(one);
  getaray(two);
  getmax(one,max,index);
  writeln('Max of first array is ',max,' at index ',index);
  getmax(two,max,index);
  writeln('Max of second array is ',max,' at index ',
    index);
end.
```

You can see in the above program an array used both as a variable parameter and as a value parameter. The procedure *getaray* uses a variable array parameter because it must pass back the array with new values in it. The procedure *getmax* uses a value parameter—it could have used a variable parameter but does not need one. However, it is always better to use a variable parameter with arrays. For every array value parameter, the computer has to devote time and space to making a copy when the procedure is called.

> *Always pass arrays as **var** parameters.*

It is easy to forget this, so always double check.

You should note that Pascal will not permit a procedure or function heading like this one:

```
procedure findmax(var iray:array[1..1Ø] of
    integer;bigone;where:integer);
```

Instead the type of the array has to be given by a type identifier. In passing a typed array by this method, the actual parameter and the formal parameter used in the procedure heading must use the same type identifier and therefore will be exactly the same size. At the end of this chapter we will see how 'conformant array parameters' can introduce some flexibility into the situation.

4 A sorting procedure—bubble sort

Sorting is the process of arranging items in order according to their value. It is a very important process, particularly in commercial computing, and there are many ways of doing it. The bubble sort is not efficient, but it is easy to understand.

Suppose we want to arrange items in ascending order. To bubble sort an array of disordered values, we scan through the array exchanging each item with its neighbour to get the larger of the two values further up the array. After one such pass, the array is more ordered and we can be sure that the largest item has been carried to the end of the array. Now the next pass can stop one before the end, and so on. In its simplest form we make $n-1$ passes at an array of length n items.

Earlier in this course we saw a procedure *ordure* to examine two items and exchange them if necessary, and this is used here by the procedure *bubsort*. Note that a member of the array is passed as a variable parameter to the procedure *ordure* by a statement like

```
ordure(ray[i],ray[i+1])
```

An indexed reference like this is a suitable variable or value for an actual parameter if the array member is of the correct type, integer in this case. This program uses random numbers to test the bubble sort procedure:

```
program bubble;

  {Test a bubble sorting procedure using
              random integers}

  const max=1Ø;

  type sortarray=array[1..max] of integer;

  var bignum:integer;   {Global needed by generator}
      iray:sortarray;
      index:integer;

  function ran(range:integer):integer;

    {A function to generate a pseudorandom
     integer in the range 1 to range

     The global variable bignum is required
     and must be initialized to an odd value}

    const mplyer=15625;

    begin
      {Get next huge number}
      bignum:=bignum*mplyer mod maxint;
      {Keep them positive}
      if bignum<Ø then bignum:=bignum+maxint;
      {And keep them odd}
      if not odd(bignum) then bignum:=bignum+1;
      {Finally the result}
      ran:=trunc(1+range*(bignum/maxint))
    end;

  procedure ordure(var x,y:integer);

    {A procedure to order parameters x and y so
        that x<=y. If x=y they are not switched.}

    var t:integer;     {Local to this procedure}
    begin
      writeln('Ordure has  ',x,y);
      if x>y then
        begin
          writeln('Switching');
          t:=x;  x:=y;  y:=t
        end;
    end;
```

```
procedure bubsort(var ray:sortarray;size:integer);

{Bubble sort of the array ray length size}

var i,top:integer;

begin
  for top:=size-1 downto 1 do
    begin
      for i:=1 to top do ordure(ray[i],ray[i+1]);
      writeln('After pass ',size-top);
      for i:=1 to size do write(ray[i]);
      writeln
    end
end;

{Main program}

begin

  bignum:=33;   {seed for randoms}

  {Make random array in range 1 to 99}

  for index:=1 to max do iray[index]:=ran(99);
  writeln;
  writeln('Here is the array before sorting');
  for index:=1 to max do write(iray[index]);
  writeln;
  bubsort(iray,max);
  writeln;
  writeln('Here is the array after sorting');
  for index:=1 to max do write(iray[index]);
end.
```

Exercise Another kind of sort is the insertion sort. To sort into ascending order, the idea is to insert one test value at a time in part of the array which is already in order. Scan along the ordered part until you find a value which is greater than the test value you are trying to insert. Then shift the entire array up one place to make room for the test value which you now insert. Begin by inserting the second value into an array fragment which consists of the first value. Then you insert the third value into an array of length two, and so on. Do this.

5 Quicksort is recursive

And it's fast, too, at least when the array is fairly disordered. The hardest part to understand about quicksort is not the recursive part. Suppose what we want is to sort an array into ascending order. Can we find exactly where a test member of the array belongs while it is still disordered? Can we do this without scanning the array more than once? Yes, we can. We have to place the test value so that everything on its left is less than or equal to it, and similarly everything on its right is greater than or equal.

Consider this array, and set index pointers *less* and *more* initially at the ends of the array. We are going to put 69 in its correct position:

less									*more*
69	32	94	97	22	84	40	79	35	71

The index *less* points to a place in the array that is either to the left of the correct position, or at it. This is true at the beginning because it is fully left. Similarly *more* is either to to the right, or correct.

We start by moving *more* to the left until we find something less than the test value 69 (this could happen at the beginning). When this happens, we exchange the values pointed at by *more* and *less*, giving in this example:

less								*more*	
35	32	94	97	22	84	40	79	69	71

Now we move *less* to the right until we find a value that is greater than our test value. Switching again we will get:

		less						*more*	
35	32	69	97	22	84	40	79	94	71

Keep moving *more* and *less* until *more* = *less*. If you follow it through you will see that eventually we have:

				less *more*					
35	32	40	22	69	84	97	79	94	71

Magically, the value 69 is in the correct place, and furthermore every value to the left or right is on the correct side of it!

So here is the action part of an procedure to do this for a fragment of an array *iray* from *min* to *max*. It places *iray*[*min*] in the correct place and tells us where in the variable place. You can see that it really is quite straightforward:

```
begin

  {Set up pointers}

  test:=iray[min];
  more:=max;
  less:=min;

  {Do the rearrangement}
```

```
    while more>less do
      begin
        while (more>less) and (test<=iray[more]) do
          more:=more-1;
        if more<>less then switch;
        while (more>less) and (test>=iray[less]) do
          less:=less+1;
        if more>less then switch;
      end;
    place:=more
end;
```

If we did this for *min* from 1 to the end of the array, it would get sorted but it would not be much faster than the bubble sort. However, after one number is in the correct place, we have two smaller disordered array framents on either side of it which we sort. Sorting two fragments is much faster than sorting a whole array. Each sort produces smaller fragments until we are finished. This does it recursively:

```
    procedure quiksort(var iray:sortarray;start,finish:integer);

    {Quicksort of the array from start to finish}

    var where:integer;

    begin
      if start<finish then
        begin

          {First place iray[start]}

          placeone(iray,start,finish,where);

          {Then quicksort the left and right fragments}

          quiksort(iray,start,where-1);
          quiksort(iray,where+1,finish)
        end
    end;
```

Here is a complete program to test quicksort and show you how it happens. In the display you can see the fragment which is being rearranged pointed at by little arrows, and the positions of *less* and *more* indicated by L and M. Don't be frightened by its length—much of it is concerned with generating random numbers and organizing the display. Nice.

```
    program shazam;

    {Demonstrate the amazing Captain Quicksort}

    const size=10;
    type sortarray=array[1..size] of integer;
```

```
var ray:sortarray;
    index:integer;
    bignum:integer;    {Global for random number generator}

function ran(range:integer):integer;
  {A function to generate a pseudorandom
   integer in the range 1 to range
   The global variable bignum is required
   and must be initialized to an odd value}
  const mplyer=15625;
  begin
    {Get next huge number}
    bignum:=bignum*mplyer mod maxint;
    {Keep them positive}
    if bignum<0 then bignum:=bignum+maxint;
    {And keep them odd}
    if not odd(bignum) then bignum:=bignum+1;
    {Finally the result}
    ran:=trunc(1+range*(bignum/maxint))
  end;

procedure placeone( var iray:sortarray;min,max:integer;
                                var place:integer);
  {Find the final position between min and max
   inclusive for the array member iray[min] so
   that it is in final sorted position with
   all less or equal members below it and all
   greater or equal members above it}

  {The procedure has a built in display}

  var less,more,test:integer;

  procedure switch;
    {Internal procedure exchanges iray[more]
             with iray[less] }
    var hold:integer;
    begin
      hold:=iray[more];
      iray[more]:=iray[less];
      iray[less]:=hold
    end;

  procedure showray;
    {Show the array and indicate the positions
         of min, less, more, and max}
    var i:integer;
    begin
      writeln;
      for i:=1 to size do write(iray[i]:5);
      writeln;
```

```
      for i:=4 to (min)*5 do write(' '); write('∧');
      for i:=1 to (less-min)*5 do write(' '); write('L');
      for i:=1 to (more-less)*5 do write(' ');write('M');
      for i:=1 to (max-more)*5 do write(' '); write('∧');
      writeln;
    end;

  {Here is the action part of Placeone}
  begin
    {Set up pointers}
    test:=iray[min];
    more:=max;
    less:=min;
    writeln('*********** Now do this fragment ************')
    showray;
    {Do the rearrangement}
    while more>less do
      begin
        while (more>less) and (test<=iray[more])
          do more:=more-1;
        if more<>less then switch;
        showray;
        while (more>less) and (test>=iray[less])
          do less:=less+1;
        if more>less then switch;
        showray
      end;
    place:=more
  end;

procedure quiksort(var iray:sortarray;start,finish:integer);
  {Quicksort of the array from start to finish}
  var where:integer;
  begin
    if start<finish then
      begin
        {First place iray[start]}
        placeone(iray,start,finish,where);
        {Then quicksort the left and right fragments}
        quiksort(iray,start,where-1);
        quiksort(iray,where+1,finish)
      end
  end;

{Main program}

begin
  bignum:=35;   {seed for randoms}
  {Make random array in range 1 to 99}
  for index:=1 to size do ray[index]:=ran(99);
  writeln;
```

```
writeln('Here is the array before sorting');
for index:=1 to size do write(ray[index]);
writeln;
quiksort(ray,1,size);
writeln;
writeln('Here is the array after sorting');
for index:=1 to size do write(ray[index]);
end.
```

6 Conformant array parameters

This somewhat unwieldy title describes a mechanism which allows a Pascal procedure or function to use arrays whose bounds are variable. This is an optional extension to Pascal described in the Pascal standard and it is not universally adopted. It does not completely meet the need for the passing of array fragments, and there are certain other restrictions which are likely to cause more frustration than joy in practice. Therefore I describe it here for completeness, but cannot wholeheartedly recommend it.

A procedure may include an array parameter with variable bounds in its parameter list, such as in this procedure for rotating the members of an array:

```
procedure swivel(var swivray:array[min..max:integer]
   of integer);
   {Rotate the array swivray to the left}
   var i,save:integer;
   begin
     writeln('Before');
     revealit(swivray);
     save:=swivray[1];
     for i:=min to max-1 do swivray[i]:=swivray[i+1];
     swivray[max]:=save;
     writeln('After');
     revealit(swivray)
   end;
```

The conformant array parameter is distinguished by the way its type is stated in the procedure heading:

    array[*lower bound name* .. *upper bound name* : *index type*] **of** *type name*

All elements of this description are required — in particular the bounds cannot be constants.

When the procedure is activated by a reference to it, an array of the appropriate type has to be given. The values of the lower and upper bounds are worked out and passed to the procedure, where they are available as values that can be used in expressions—but they cannot be treated as variables. Note that the index type as given in the parameter description of the **procedure** heading must be compatible with the actual index type when the array is passed. This main program uses *swivel*:

```
program conform;
  {Demonstrate conformant array parameters}
  const size=8;
  var demoray:array[1..size] of integer;

  {procedures revealit, getit and swivel go in here}

  {Main program}
  begin
    getit(demoray);
    swivel(demoray);
  end.
```

Both variable and value parameters can be used. However there is a rule that prevents a conformant array parameter being passed down to another function or procedure as a value parameter. For example, the procedure *swivel* uses something called *revealit* and passes to it the conformant array parameter *swivray*. Because of this rule, *revealit* can only have this parameter as a variable parameter. You can see in *revealit* that the procedure does not itself require a variable parameter—it does not return any new values. However, to make it available to any procedure, it is made a variable parameter.

```
procedure revealit(var ray:array[dn..up:integer] of integer);
  {Useful routine for displaying any integer array}
  var index:integer;
  begin
    writeln;
    for index:=dn to up do write(ray[index]);
    writeln
  end;
```

The procedure *getit* requires a variable parameter anyway:

```
procedure getit(var ray:array[first..last:integer]
  of integer);
  {Useful routine for inputting any integer array}
  var index:integer;
  begin
    writeln('Please enter ',last-first:3,' integer values');
    for index:=first to last do read(ray[index]);
    writeln
  end;
```

Finally the question of assignment. We found earlier in this chapter that one array could only be assigned to another provided that we used the same type identifier. With conformant array parameters, provided that two arrays share the same type name in the heading, like this:

```
function xtoy(x,y:array[foist..layst:integer] of integer);
```

it is possible to say

x : =y

However in the actual call to the procedure, *x* and *y* must be of the same type with all that implies, otherwise Pascal could not work out *foist* and *layst*.

So what are the problems? First of all, even though the procedure makes the array size adjustable, an entire array must be passed to it. Unfortunately it is not possible to pass an array fragment. Using conformant array parameters is likely to make the program slow, particularly if they are value parameters. Value array parameters are of limited usefulness anyway. Also there are restrictions which affect packed arrays and character strings, as revealed in the next chapter. Given that not all versions of Pascal allow them, conformant array parameters are of somewhat limited value. Pascal has a few serious deficiencies, and one of them is in passing array parameters.

7 Problems

Problem 12.1 One interesting fact about Pascal's triangle is that each number in the triangle is the sum of the two above it as it is written. Formally, this means that

$$_nC_r = {}_{n-1}C_{r-1} + {}_{n-1}C_r$$

Write a program to make Pascal's triangle using this fact. Use an array to represent a row of the triangle and recompute the new row from the old one each time. It can be done with or without recursion. I prefer it without.

Problem 12.2 One quick way to find prime numbers is by 'sieving'. Set up a long array

```
sieve:array[1..length] of integer
```

in which you define $sieve[i] = i$. Now work along the array from $sieve[2]$. Whenever you find a non-zero value in the array, set all its multiples to zero but not the value itself. When you have reached $sieve[trunc(sqrt(length))]$, all the non-zero numbers in the array are prime! Write a program to do this, and then see what improvements you can make. How big will your computer allow *length* to be?

Problem 12.3 An array can be used to make a histogram which counts the occurrences of events. A good way to demonstrate this is by simulating the throwing of dice. The sum of two random integers each in the range 1 to 6 gives an integer from 2 to 12 which represents the throw of a pair of dice. If you have an array *hist*: **array**[2 . .12] **of** *integer*, initially all zeros, then you can add one to $hist[i]$ every time the throw is *i*. After a while, say 360 throws, display the values in *hist*. Are they what you expect?

Problem 12.4 In the insertion sort, and in other applications also, we have to search an array which is already in order to find where a test value should (or does) reside. The binary search is a very efficient way of doing this. By using index pointers similar to those in the quicksort program, we determine which half the value belongs in, then which quarter, which eighth, and so on until the desired index is found. Write a binary searching function, and incorporate it in the insertion sort program. This is a very 'searching' test of one's ability to think with array indices. If you're having trouble, draw a picture.

Thirteen
Characters

1 Character items and strings

The ease of manipulating characters in Pascal is one of its joys. A variable or constant of type *char* holds only one character:

```
program chico;
  const star='*';
  var show:char;
  begin
    show:=star;
    writeln('Here''s a star .. ',star)
  end.
```

Exactly what characters are available depends on the computer system. You are certain to have at least the upper case alphabet and enough special symbols to run Pascal. On small computers the character set known as ASCII (American Standard Code for Information Interchange) is nearly universal. Unfortunately the manufacturers of some large computers have their own 'standards'.

We have seen *string constants* from the beginning. Any series of characters enclosed in single quotes is a string constant, and it can contain any characters known to your computer. To include a quotation mark, put two of them:

```
writeln('To get '' you have to put ''''!')
```

Pascal allows you also to use *character string variables*, although you have to declare them as being **packed arrays of** *char* with integer indices from 1 to a particular length. A string of length 12 might be

```
charles:packed array[1..12] of char
```

The description **packed** is an instruction to Pascal to cram the characters into as little space as possible. We have not discussed the packing concept before because it is of no use with real or integer values. However when dealing with ordered types in which there are relatively few possible values, space can be saved by packing. This is true of character or boolean arrays in particular, and also of types that you may invent yourself (Chapter 15).

However, with characters, the important thing about packing is that special things can be done with a string variable, and a string variable is a **packed array**. These special things are revealed in the sections which follow, and apply particularly to assignment, comparison, and output.

2 Writing and reading characters

Writing is easy. The Pascal procedures *write* or *writeln* are able to display single characters or strings—either variables or constants. With any of these you can use a field width specification. This is an alternative form of the procedure *plunkit* defined in Chapter 9:

```
procedure plunkit(column:integer);

  {Plots a star at column column}

  begin
    if column>=2 then write(' ':column-1);
    writeln('*')
  end;
```

Reading is a bit harder. *Read* or *readln* can only get one character at a time, so to read a string you have to make a loop. This little program illustrates how a string variable may be written, and what you have to do to read it:

```
program chario;

    {Read and write a character string}

    var ch:packed array[1..5] of char;
        i:integer;

    begin
      writeln;
      write('Enter 5 characters please .. ');
      for i:= 1 to 5 do read(ch[i]);
      writeln;
      write('This is what you entered ',ch)
    end.
```

Note that only a **packed array of** *char* with integer indices and lower bound 1 is considered to be a string—a character array cannot be written without an indexing loop unless it is a string.

There is a special boolean function called *eoln* which can tell you when the end of an input line is being reached. It is normally *false* and becomes *true* when there are no more characters in an input line. If you try to read another character, you get a blank and *eoln* becomes *false* again because you are about to start into the next line. Effectively at a terminal the 'return' or 'enter' key gives you *eoln=true* just before you read it, and a blank when you do read it. This is useful when reading characters, but also presents a problem as discussed in the exercise which follows this example:

> *Example* This program has a useful procedure *readin* which will read characters into a string of length 12. However instead of giving one blank and carrying on when the user presses 'return', it fills out the string with additional blanks and tells you how many characters were entered. In this version the procedure is told a maximum number to expect, which might be less than 12:

```
program chin;

    type string12=packed array[1..12] of char;

    var ch:string12;
    lenth:integer;

    procedure readin(var instring:string12;
      var len:integer);

      {How to read a character string}

      var i:integer;

      begin
        writeln;
        write('Enter up to ',len:2,
          ' characters please .. ');
        i:=0;
        while not eoln and (i<len) do
          begin
            i:=i+1;
            read(instring[i])
          end;
        len:=i;
        for i:=i+1 to 12 do instring[i]:=' ';
        readln
      end;

    {Main program}

    begin
      lenth:=8;
      readin(ch,lenth);
      writeln('You entered ',lenth:2,' characters.');
      writeln('This is what they are .. ',ch)
    end.
```

Notice that a type identifier *string12* is used to describe a string of length 12. Remember that a type identifier is needed to be able to pass a whole array parameter to a procedure. A special rule of Pascal forbids you to pass an item from within a packed variable as a **var** parameter to a procedure or function. The *read* and *readln* procedures are exempt from this rule and so we have been able to say

```
read(instring[i])
```

We could not, however, say

```
dothis(instring[i])
```

if the procedure *dothis* was defined by

```
procedure dothis(var ch:char);
```

Exercise Now although the above program is probably well behaved, there is a snag with *eoln* if you are working interactively at a terminal. Suppose you are going to enter an empty line. The *eoln* has to be true before you do—can Pascal read your mind? Clearly impossible. Different Pascal implementations deal with this in different ways. One that I know regards an empty line as one blank. This one would incorrectly give you length 1 for an empty line and also 1 if the line had only one character in the above program. This means that you cannot distinguish an empty line from a line that really contains just one blank. Another that I know changes the definition of *eoln* so that you get it *true* with the blank rather than before it. This may be more helpful, but it violates the Pascal standard. The above program would always give you the length as being one greater than it should on such a system.

So what are you supposed to do? Make the above program fill out with '*' rather than blanks and use it to find out what your Pascal does about *eoln* on an interactive terminal.

3 Conformant parameters with strings

Although paradoxically a conformant array parameter can never be a string, it can be very useful in dealing with packed arrays of characters. This procedure can read a string of any length:

```
procedure strin(var strang:packed array[min..max:integer]
   of char);

   {Read any string or for that matter
      any packed array of char}

   var i:integer;
      ch:char;

   begin
     writeln('Please enter ',max—min+1:2,' characters .. ');
     for i:=min to max do
       begin
         read(ch);
         strang[i]:=ch
       end
end;
```

and this next one can write a string of any length although it has to do it character by character. Why? Because *strang* is not really a string—strings have a lower bound of 1, not *min*. Therefore *strang* cannot be passed as a string to the procedure *write*. Also *strang* is a variable parameter to avoid trouble with the rule that prevents value conformant array parameters from being passed down through several layers of procedures.

```
procedure strout(var strang:packed array[min..max:integer]
    of char);

{Display any string or likewise any packed array of char}

{Note that the display is made on the current line}

var i:integer;
    ch:character;

begin
  for i:=min to max do
    begin
      ch:=strang[i];
      write(ch)
    end
end;
```

4 Using characters

A character value can be assigned to a character variable:

```
ch:='*'
```

As there are no operations that produce a character result, the right hand side of this assignment can only be a character variable or constant, or the result of a function of type *char*. You might write a character function of your own, or use the *chr*, *succ* or *pred* functions of Pascal.

Similarly a string value can be assigned to a string variable, but only if they use exactly the same type identifier, which implies that they are the same length. We will discuss how we might get around this with our own useful function for assigning and concatenating strings of apparently different lengths shortly.

The type *char* is an ordered type of Pascal. This means that any given symbol has a correct place in the order. Unfortunately you cannot rely on the order to be the same from one computer to the next. We can, however, say a few things about this.

(i)   The most likely order is the ASCII code, which is listed in the Appendix.

(ii)   You can rely on the upper case letters to be themselves in order, with 'A' before 'B' and so on. However, they may not be consecutive.

(iii) 'A' and 'a' will not have the same code, which raises an interesting problem in arranging things in alphabetical order.

(iv)   You can rely on the the lower case letters to be themselves in order (if they are available) with 'a' before 'b' and so on. However, they may not be consecutive.

(v)   You can rely on the digits '0' to '9' to be in order. However, they may not be consecutive.

Some built-in functions of Pascal are useful with characters.

ord(*character value*)
> gives the integer result which is the position of the character in the computer's sequence.

chr(*integer value*)
> gives the character result which is the character whose position is given by the *integer value*.

> For example, in ASCII *ord*('A') is 65 and *chr*(65) is 'A'. *Ord* and *chr* always work in this complementary way.

succ(*character value*)
> gives the next character in sequence. For example, *succ*('a') should be 'b'. *Succ* means 'successor'.

pred(*character value*)
> gives the previous character in sequence. For example, *pred*('z') should be 'y'. *Pred* means 'predecessor'.

Because the character type is ordered, it can be used as an index counter in a **for** loop.

```
for ch:='a' to 'z' do write(ord(ch))
```

and it can also be used as the index of an array:

```
var chray:array['a'..'z'] of integer
```

Furthermore a character (but not a string) can be used as a **case** selector. We will use this in an example later in this chapter.

> *Exercise* Write a program which displays as nicely as you can both the position and character value of all the characters on your computer. You may have to discover the range by experimentation. In ASCII all codes from 32 to 127 are printable characters.

> *Example* Although Pascal cannot do variable length strings, a common way to simulate these is to work with long strings. These strings always hold useful characters at the beginning and are filled out at the end with some character.

This program contains procedures to read and write a 'dynamic string' along with a procedure for concatenation, meaning splicing two strings together. The actual fixed string length used, 132 in this program, is a bit arbitrary but is a fairly common maximum width for lineprinters and better printing terminals.

```
program dynastring;

{Demonstrates how variable length strings can be
 achieved. The '~' is sacrificed as a filler. }

const stringmax=132;

type dynamic=packed array[1..stringmax] of char;

var one,two,three:dynamic;

procedure readastr(var instr:dynamic);

  {Ask the user to enter a dynamic string}

  var i:integer;
      ch:char;

  begin
    writeln;
    writeln('Enter a string not ending with ''~'' .. ');
    i:=0;
    while (not eoln) and (i<stringmax) do
      begin
        i:=i+1;
        read(ch);
        instr[i]:=ch
      end;
    for i:=i+1 to stringmax do instr[i]:='~'; {***}
    readln;
  end;

procedure showastr(var shstr:dynamic);

  {Display a dynamic string}

  var i:integer;
      ch:char;

  begin
    i:=1;
    while (i<stringmax) and (shstr[i]<>'~') do
      begin
        ch:=shstr[i];
        write(ch);
        i:=i+1
      end
  end;
```

```
procedure concat(left,right:dynamic; var result:dynamic);

   {Concatenate two dynamic strings. Fill with '~'
    if combined length < stringmax, truncate if >  }

   var i,j:integer;
       ch:char;

   begin

      {First copy left string}

      i:=0;
      repeat
        i:=i+1;
        ch:=left[i];
        result[i]:=ch;
      until (ch='~') or (i=stringmax);

      {Now right string until out of room}

      if ch='~' then
        begin
          j:=1;
          while i<stringmax do
            begin
              result[i]:=right[j];
              i:=i+1; j:=j+1
            end
        end;
   end;
```

{Main program to try this}

```
                                    begin
                                      readastr(one); readastr(two);
                                      concat(one,two,three);
                                      showastr(three)
                                    end.
```

Exercise If you are interested in using strings, the procedures in the above program may be helpful to you. Get it to work, and check that it gives the results you expect. It is possible that you will get an unwanted space from the procedure *readastr*—if the *eoln* function has been implemented strangely on your machine. If it does, change the line marked {***} to

```
for i:=i to stringmax instr[i]:='~'
```

Now write a function

```
function lenstr(strung:dynamic):integer;
```

which tells you the effective length of the dynamic string *strung*.

There is more to do with dynamic strings in the problems at the end of this chapter, and there is also another approach altogether using the record type in Chapter 16 which is used in several data structures in Chapter 18.

5 Comparing characters—and case selection, too

You might well wish to compare characters. The result of a comparison depends on the order of character codes in your computer.

Example The hexadecimal (base 16) number system is often used in computers because there is a direct relation between its digits and the organization of items stored in a computer. In hexadecimal, the decimal digits from 0 to 15 are coded as follows:

Decimal	*Hexadecimal*	*Decimal*	*Hexadecimal*
0	0	8	8
1	1	9	9
2	2	10	A
3	3	11	B
4	4	12	C
5	5	13	D
6	6	14	E
7	7	15	F

The digits differ in the range A to F. The next number after F in hexadecimal is 10. A hexadecimal number with two digits has this interpretation:

$$3 \qquad E$$

Sixteens   Units

so that the value shown, 3E, is the same as $3 \times 16 + 14$ or 62 in decimal. A byte of a computer's memory can (usually) have its value expressed as two hexadecimal digits, from 00 to FF. This corresponds to the positive integers 0 to 255.

This procedure computes the positive integer value of two hexadecimal digits, using the *ord* function to compute the decimal digits. The string type *hexbyte* is used for the hexadecimal value.

```
type hexbyte=packed array[1..2] of char;
```

```
procedure decit(hex:hexbyte; var dec:integer);

    {Convert hebyte hex to decimal integer dec}

    var i:integer;
    ch:char;
```

```
begin
  dec:=∅;
  for i:=1 to 2 do
    begin
      ch:=hex[i];
      if (ch>='∅') and (ch<='9') then
        dec:=dec*16+ord(ch)-ord('∅')
      else if (ch>='A') and (ch<='F') then
        dec:=dec*16+ord(ch)-ord('A')+1∅
          else dec:=999;
    end
end;
```

This one uses a **case** structure, not because it's efficient, but to illustrate it:

```
procedure hexit(dec:integer; var hex:hexbyte);

{Convert decimal dec to hexbyte hex}

var ch:char;
    i,digit:integer;

begin
  for i:=2 downto 1 do
    begin
      digit:=dec mod 16;
      dec:=dec div 16;
      case digit of
        ∅: ch:='∅'; 1: ch:='1'; 2: ch:='2';
        3: ch:='3'; 4: ch:='4'; 5: ch:='5';
        6: ch:='6'; 7: ch:='7'; 8: ch:='8';
        9: ch:='9'; 1∅:ch:='A'; 11:ch:='B';
        12: ch:='C'; 13:ch:='D'; 14:ch:='E';
        15: ch:='F'
      end;
      hex[i]:=ch
    end
end;
```

Exercise Do *decit* with a **case** structure, and *hexit* without one. *Decit* requires upper case hexadecimal characters. Modify it to do either upper or lower case.

6 Comparing strings

You can directly compare string values provided they are exactly the same length.

Because strings are compared from left to right, the ordering of character values ensures that

'ABC' < 'ABD'   is *true*

However the codes of upper case and lower case letters are not the same. Because of variations between versions of Pascal it is not possible to predict whether or not

'ZZZ' < 'aaa'

(although in ASCII it is true). The space is also ambiguous. In ASCII

'ABC ' < 'ABCA'

Example You might think that alphabetical ordering is impossible because 'A' is not the same as 'a'. Do not despair! Here is a procedure which does it for a dynamic string. You can see that this is a stringy version of *ordure*, and so has implications for sorting! The strings to be compared are first converted to local upper case values:

```
procedure chordure(var ch1,ch2:dynamic);

   {Very pleasing procedure to ordure the
    dynamic strings ch1 and ch2}

   var lc1,lc2:dynamic;
       i:integer;

    procedure shifty(var shstr:dynamic);

       {Shift dynamic string to upper case}

       var i:integer;
           ch:char;

       begin
         i:=1;
         while (shstr[i]<>'~') and (i<stringmax) do
           begin
             ch:=shstr[i];
             if (ch>='a') and (ch<='z') then
                shstr[i]:=chr(ord('A')+ord(ch)-ord('a'));
             i:=i+1
           end
       end;   {End of shifty}

   {Action part of chordure}

   begin
     lc1:=ch1;
     shifty(lc1);
     lc2:=ch2;                        begin
     shifty(lc2);                        lc1:=ch2;
     if lc1>lc2 then                     ch2:=ch1;
                                         ch1:=lc1
                                      end
                                    end;
```

Exercise The behaviour of *chordure* for dynamic strings whose effective lengths are different cannot be predicted in general. This has to do with the choice of filler character. So why was the space not used as a filler in the first place? Without using a different filler, correct *chordure* to make it work in any Pascal implementation which has upper and lower case letters. Also investigate the behaviour of blanks, and ensure that 'bye bye' is less than 'byebye '. Some of the procedures given earlier for dynamic strings will help you.

7 Anagrams can be recursive

An anagram is a rearrangement of the letters of one word to spell another. Puzzle people may find it helpful to have a computer program to display all the possible rearrangements. It can be done as a series of nested loops, but this is difficult to program well if the number of letters is to be adjustable.

The recursive approach is better. To list the angrams when the number of letters is *nchars*, we take each letter in turn as the final one and work out all the angrams of the *nchars*−1 preceding ones, for example if the word is 'spot', we find

	the anagrams of spo	followed by t
	the anagrams of tsp	followed by o
	the anagrams of ots	followed by p
and	the anagrams of pot	followed by s

I am sure that you can see that the final letter is selected by rotating the original word. So this is what we do:

```
procedure magrana(nchars:integer);

  {This procedure makes the anagrams of length nchars}

  var i,j:integer;
  begin
    if nchars>1 then
      for i:=1 to nchars do
        begin

          {Make all anagrams of length nchars — 1}

          magrana(nchars—1);

          {and get all rotations of length nchars}

          rotate(nchars)
        end
    else showray
  end;
```

In the above, *rotate* is a procedure to rotate the characters, and *showray* displays each anagram. After each set of anagrams the original word is back in order, and so the process works correctly. Here, in a full implementation, the global character array *annie* is used for the anagrams:

```
program anagram;

    {A program to do anagrams}

    var annie:array[1..1Ø] of char;
        i,inchars:integer;
        chin:char;

    procedure showray;

    {Display the array}

      var i:integer;
      begin
        for i:=1 to inchars do write (annie[i]);
        writeln
      end;

    procedure rotate(nrot:integer);

      {Rotate the array right one character}

      var i:integer;
          c:char;
      begin
        c:=annie[1];
        for i:=1 to nrot-1 do
          annie[i]:=annie[i+1];
        annie[nrot]:=c;
      end;

    procedure magrana(nchars:integer);

      {This procedure makes the anagrams of length nchars}

      var i,j:integer;
      begin
        if nchars>1 then
          for i:=1 to nchars do
            begin

                {Make all anagrams of length nchars - 1}

                magrana(nchars-1);

                {and get all rotations of length nchars}
```

```
        rotate(nchars)
      end
    else showray
  end;

{Main program}

begin
  writeln('This program finds all anagrams');
  write('of up to 9 letters. Enter a word .. ');
  inchars:=∅;
  while (not eoln) and (inchars<1∅) do
    begin
      read(chin);              writeln;
      inchars:=inchars+1;      writeln('Here are the anagrams');
      annie[inchars]:=chin     inchars:=inchars-1;
    end;                       if inchars>∅ then magrana(inchars)
                             end.
```

8 Problems

Problem 13.1 For hexadecimal numbers create a procedure which accepts a string of variable length from the terminal and converts it to an integer value. That is not too difficult until you hit a hexadecimal number which represents a negative value. Can you make it work over the full integer range? If you can, it will show you how your computer represents negative numbers. Helpful hint: on many small computers FFFF in hexadecimal is actually −1.

Problem 13.2 Using what you have learned from Problem 13.1, create procedures which:

(i)   Display the hexadecimal value of any integer.

(ii) Display the binary value of any integer.

(iii) Display the binary value of a hexadecimal string.

Problem 13.3 When you run the anagram program given in this chapter, you will see that it is not easy to follow the anagrams visually if your display is on a screen. This is because you read from left to right, while it is the rightmost character that is most stable. It would be better the other way round. Do it.

Problem 13.4 This chapter introduced the 'dynamic string' which is not a Pascal feature, but one that we program into it. Create procedures which, given a dynamic string:

(i)   Insert a specified string at a specified position in a dynamic string.

(ii) Delete a specified number of characters beginning at a specified position in a dynamic string.

(iii) Replace part of a dynamic string with a specified string beginning at a specified position.

Fourteen
Arrays of arrays

1 Arrays with more subscripts

In Pascal there are two ways of using arrays with more than one index. In this section, we see the traditional way, similar to other computer languages, in which one simply uses more indices. In the next section, it will be seen that the concept of an array of arrays allows some interesting things to be done.

You can use extra indices simply by defining the array to have them, either by expressing their ranges in the **var** declaration, as in

```
var table:array[1..4,1..6] of real;
```

or by creating a type with more than one index, and using it:

```
type cube=array[1..3,1..3,1..3] of integer;
var tictactoe:cube;
```

Example Over a five year period, the four cities of Grotsylvania have kept records of the occurrence of parking meter vandalism, with the following results:

Parking Meters Vandalized

Year	Northminster	Southleigh	Eastchester	Westhampton
1	35	226	191	21
2	163	45	338	335
3	228	281	42	187
4	121	264	109	143
5	182	370	16	17

In Pascal, we could easily represent this information in an array of two dimensions:

```
var destroyed:array[1..5,1..4] of integer;
```

in which the first index represents the year, and is therefore the row number in the table, while the second is the column number. We want to make a little Pascal program to work out the year and district totals. This brings us into contact with an unfortunate omission from the Pascal language; there is no way of giving initial values to the array, or indeed to any variable. We must either set up the table through a series of assignment statements, or we must read it in from a file which is created in some other way. Here, assignments are used. To read from a file, consult Chapter 17.

```
program parking;

   {Demonstrates the use of two subscripts
      with a single array identifier}

   {The illustration is a table of incidences of parking
      meter vandalism in four cities over five years}

   var tbl:array[1..5,1..4] of integer;
       yearsums:array[1..5] of integer;
       citysums:array[1..4] of integer;
       bigsum:integer;
       city,year:integer;

   begin

      {Set up the table by assignment}

      tbl[1,1]:=35;   tbl[1,2]:=226;
      tbl[1,3]:=191;  tbl[1,4]:=21;
      tbl[2,1]:=163;  tbl[2,2]:=45;
      tbl[2,3]:=338;  tbl[2,4]:=335;
      tbl[3,1]:=228;  tbl[3,2]:=281;
      tbl[3,3]:=42;   tbl[3,4]:=187;
      tbl[4,1]:=121;  tbl[4,2]:=264;
      tbl[4,3]:=109;  tbl[4,4]:=143;
      tbl[5,1]:=182;  tbl[5,2]:=370;
      tbl[5,3]:=16;   tbl[5,4]:=17;

      {Do the yearly sums}

      for year:=1 to 5 do
        begin
          yearsums[year]:=0;
          for city:=1 to 4 do
            yearsums[year]:=yearsums[year]+tbl[year,city]
        end;

      {Show the table and the row sums}

      writeln;
      writeln('·              Parking Meter Vandalism');
      writeln;
      write('      Year    North    South');
      writeln('    East      West      Total');
      for year:=1 to 5 do
        begin
          write(year:8);
          for city:=1 to 4 do write(tbl[year,city]:8);
          writeln(yearsums[year]:8)
        end;
```

```
{Do the city sums}

for city:=1 to 4 do
  begin
    citysums[city]:=0;
    for year:=1 to 5 do
      citysums[city]:=citysums[city]+tbl[year,city];
  end;


{Show the city sums}

writeln;
write('  Totals');
for city:=1 to 4 do write(citysums[city]:8);

{Do the big sum and show it}

bigsum:=0;
for city:=1 to 4 do bigsum:=bigsum+citysums[city];
writeln(bigsum:8)
end.
```

Exercise You can do this in fewer loops, and furthermore either or both of the one dimensional arrays *citysums* and *yearsums* can be eliminated, depending on how many loops you compress. And there are no procedures. Improve this program.

In general, an array can have any number of subscripts, and the subscripts could be of different types as long as, like any index, they are an ordered type such as *integer* or *char*, or one you invent yourself. This is an array type:

array[*indexrange,indexrange,* . . .] **of** *datatype*

Arrays can be **packed**. Packing is a feature which depends on the computer being used. Its intention is to save space in the computer's memory by packing items as closely as possible, although it may or may not result in a saving. If packing does result in a saving of memory, it also usually slows a program down:

packed array[*indexrange,* . . .] **of** *datatype*

You are not allowed to pass an item from within a packed array to a procedure as a **var** parameter. The *read* and *readln* procedures are an exception—you can, for example, ask them to read a single character into a string.

2 Arrays of arrays

There is no reason why the data type that is made into an array cannot itself be an array, for example:

```
const  listmax=2ØØ;    {We have to be able to fit}
       stringmax=24;   {all of this into memory}
       quitstring='Finished~~~~~~~~~~~~~~~~';
                            {24 characters}

type   dynamic=packed array[1..stringmax] of char;
       list=array[1..listmax] of dynamic;

var    sortlist:list;
       finished:boolean;
       num,i:integer;
```

Using this arangement, *sortlist* is an array of packed arrays of characters—in other words an array of strings. To refer to a particular string we would use one index, as in

```
tempstring:=sortlist[index]
```

We can also get an individual character if we want it, using

```
onechar:=sortlist[index][number]
```

In other words, *sortlist[index]* is a value of type *dynamic*, while *sortlist[index][number]* refers to a single character within it. Of course *index* and *number* must each have values in the permitted range for that particular index.

We are allowed to assign either whole arrays of the same type:

```
anotherlist:=sortlist
```

or whole strings:

```
tempstring:=sortlist[index]
```

or individual characters:

```
onechar:=sortlist[index][number]
```

Any of these can also be passed as a value parameter to a procedure or function, as we will see in the next section. *Sortlist[index][number]* cannot be passed on its own as a var parameter because it is an item from within a packed array. You will recall, however, that the only array type that can be written using the normal output stream (probably your screen) is a **packed array of** *char*. We will see how to write other array structures to special files in Chapter 17.

3 Array structures and procedures

To pass an array to a procedure, it must it must be created using a type identifier which is the same as the type of the parameter in the **procedure** declaration. This means that only whole arrays can be passed, although on some computers the use of conformant array parameters can allow you to pass different whole arrays of different sizes.

A structure which is an array of arrays allows you to pass any level of its structure provided that level is described by a type identifier which you have declared. You cannot, however, pass an item from inside a packed structure as a **var** parameter.

> *Example* In Chapter 13 we invented dynamic strings, which were padded out with the symbol '~' so that we could pretend to process strings of variable length. Here we use this idea to sort a list of strings into order, as you might do in preparing an index. The procedures *readastr*, *showastr* and *chordure* are imported from Chapter 13, along with a new one which bubble sorts a list of dynamic strings.

```
program indexer;

   {Demonstrates passing of structured array types}

   const listmax=200;    {We have to be able to fit}
         stringmax=24;   {all of this into memory}
         quitstring='Finished~~~~~~~~~~~~~~~~';
               {24 Characters}

   type  dynamic=packed array[1..stringmax] of char;
         list=array[1..listmax] of dynamic;

   var   sortlist:list;
         finished:boolean;
         num,i:integer;

procedure readastr(var instr:dynamic);

   {This procedure is from Chapter 13}


procedure showastr(var shstr:dynamic);

   {This procedure is from Chapter 13}

procedure chordure(var ch1,ch2:dynamic);

   {This procedure is from Chapter 13}

procedure bubstr(number:integer);

   {Bubble sort number entries in the global list sortlist}
```

```
    var i,top:integer;

    begin
      for top:=number-1 downto 1 do
        for i:=1 to top do
          chordure(sortlist[i],sortlist[i+1])
    end;


{Main program to make this index}

begin

  {Issue user friendly instructions}

  writeln('We are going to make an index.');
  writeln;
  writeln('Enter the lines of your index one at a time.');
  writeln('For example ..');
  writeln;
  writeln('Minkowski''s inequality 91');
  writeln;
  writeln('When you are finished, enter ''Finished''');
  writeln('Big F, little i ...');
  writeln;

  {Read in the list}

  num:=1;
  finished:=false;
  repeat
    readastr(sortlist[num]);
    if sortlist[num]=quitstring then finished:=true
      else num:=num+1
  until finished or (num>listmax);

  {Sort it}

  writeln('Thank you, sorting it now ..');
  num:=num-1;
  if num>1 then bubstr(num);

  {And finally show it}

  writeln('Here is your index:');
  for i:=1 to num do
    begin
      showastr(sortlist[i]);
      writeln
    end
end.
```

Observe the passing of the entire list to *bubstr* after it has been built up interactively, and then the passing of individual strings to *chordure*. To make it work, you have to cope with the ordering difficulty that *chordure* has with strings of different length which are the same up to the end of the shorter one, for example 'ab' and 'abc'. This was an exercise in Chapter 13. Be sure that you have the correct version of *readastr* for the implementation of *eoln* on your computer.

4 Equations (and matrices)

Arrays of two dimensions are often used to represent either systems of linear equations or matrices, so a brief introduction to each is given in this section and the next one. A series of equations like this one:

$$a + b + c = 12$$
$$a + 2b + 1.5c = 18.5$$
$$2a + 1.5b + 3c = 27$$

can be represented in mathematical shorthand using arrays. The two dimensional array:

$$A = \begin{pmatrix} 1 & 1 & 1 \\ 1 & 2 & 1.5 \\ 2 & 1.5 & 3 \end{pmatrix} = \begin{pmatrix} a_{11} & a_{12} & a_{13} \\ a_{21} & a_{22} & a_{23} \\ a_{31} & a_{32} & a_{33} \end{pmatrix}$$

represents the coefficients of the equations, and the array

$$y = \begin{pmatrix} 12 \\ 18.5 \\ 27 \end{pmatrix} = \begin{pmatrix} y_1 \\ y_2 \\ y_3 \end{pmatrix}$$

represents the right hand side. Indeed the whole system of equations can be represented by the matrix equation

$$Ax = y$$

if $$\qquad x = \begin{pmatrix} x_1 \\ x_2 \\ x_3 \end{pmatrix} = \begin{pmatrix} a \\ b \\ c \end{pmatrix}$$

is the array of unknowns.

When equations are solved by hand, variables are eliminated in turn to give smaller sets of equations. This could be done systematically. If the equations are

$$a_{11}x_1 + a_{12}x_2 + a_{13}x_3 = y_1 \qquad (1)$$
$$a_{21}x_1 + a_{22}x_2 + a_{23}x_3 = y_2 \qquad (2)$$
$$a_{31}x_1 + a_{32}x_2 + a_{33}x_3 = y_3 \qquad (3)$$

then the variable x_1 can be eliminated from equation (2) by subtracting equation (1) times a_{21}/a_{11} from equation (2). Similarly subtracting a_{31}/a_{11} times (1) from (2) removes x_1 from equation (3). This gives a new set of equations:

$$a_{11}x_1 + a_{12}x_2 + a_{13}x_3 = y_1 \qquad (1)$$
$$b_{22}x_2 + b_{23}x_2 = y_2' \qquad (4)$$
$$b_{32}x_2 + b_{33}x_3 = y_3' \qquad (5)$$

Now we can remove x_2 from equation (5) by subtracting $b_{32}/b_{22}*(4)$ from it to give one more new equation:

$$a_{11}x_1 + a_{12}x_2 + a_{13}x_3 = y_1 \qquad (1)$$
$$b_{22}x_2 + b_{23}x_3 = y_2' \qquad (4)$$
$$c_{33}x_3 = y_3'' \qquad (6)$$

This method is called Gaussian elimination after the mathematician Gauss, who does not (yet) have a computer language named after him. To do this in Pascal, the array of coefficients and the array of values on the right hand side are transformed twice:

$$\begin{pmatrix} a_{11} & a_{12} & a_{13} \\ a_{21} & a_{22} & a_{23} \\ a_{31} & a_{32} & a_{33} \end{pmatrix} \quad \text{☞} \quad \begin{pmatrix} a_{11} & a_{12} & a_{13} \\ 0 & b_{22} & b_{23} \\ 0 & 0 & b_{33} \end{pmatrix} \quad \text{☞} \quad \begin{pmatrix} a_{11} & a_{12} & a_{13} \\ 0 & b_{22} & b_{23} \\ 0 & 0 & b_{33} \end{pmatrix}$$

$$\begin{pmatrix} y_1 \\ y_2 \\ y_3 \end{pmatrix} \quad \text{☞} \quad \begin{pmatrix} y_1 \\ y_2' \\ y_3' \end{pmatrix} \quad \text{☞} \quad \begin{pmatrix} y_1 \\ y_2' \\ y_3'' \end{pmatrix}$$

Once this is done, the solution is found by working backwards through the equations and substituting what we know of the solution—this is called back-substitution:

$$x_3 = y_3''/c_{33}$$
$$x_2 = (y_2' - b_{23}x_3)/b_{22}$$
$$x_1 = (y_1 - a_{12}x_2 - a_{13}x_3)/a_{11}$$

In Pascal, let us suppose we have

```
const n=4; {No. of equations}

type gaussarray=array[1..n,1..n] of real;
     vector=array[1..n] of real;

var a:gaussarray;
    x,y:vector;
```

then a procedure *gaussolve* can easily be constructed:

```
procedure gaussolve(var a:gaussarray; var x,y:vector);

{Solve n simultaneous linear equations
     by Gaussian elimination without pivoting}
```

```
      var column:integer;

      begin
        for column:=1 to n-1 do eliminate(a,y,column);
        backsub(a,x,y);
      end;
```

which uses the procedure *eliminate*:

```
      procedure eliminate(var a:gaussarray; var y:vector;
        corner:integer);

      {Remove coefficients in corner column below corner row}

      var row:integer;
          index:integer;
          pivot:real;

      begin
        for row:=corner +1 to n do
          begin
            pivot:=a[row,corner]/a[corner,corner];
            y[row]:=y[row]-pivot*y[corner];
            for index:=corner to n do
              a[row,index]:=a[row,index]-pivot*a[corner,index];
          end
      end;
```

and the back-substitution:

```
      procedure backsub(var a:gaussarray;var x,y:vector);

      {Obtain the solution x after elimination}

      var row,column:integer;
          sum:real;

      begin
        for row:=n downto 1 do
          begin
            sum:=y[row];
            for column:=row+1 to n do
              sum:=sum-a[row,column]*x[column];
            x[row]:=sum/a[row,row]
          end
      end;
```

Exercise Make this work. Pick a suitable set of equations and arrange to display the progress of the elimination process as it proceeds.

5 Matrices (and equations)

An array of one dimension can be considered to be a vector. Whether it is a row or column vector depends on your own interpretation. It is easy to write a function for the inner product of two vectors:

$$innerproduct = \sum_{k=1}^{n} x_k y_k$$

Using the definition

```
type vector=array[1..size] of real;
```

a Pascal function for the inner product is

```
function innerproduct(var x,y:vector):real;

  {Find the inner product of x and y}

  var sum:real;
      index:integer;

  begin
    sum:=0;
    for index:=1 to size do sum:=sum+x[index]*y[index];
    innerproduct:=sum
  end;
```

An *m* by *n* matrix could either be an array of two dimensions

```
type amatrix=array[1..height,1..width];
```

or it could be an array of vectors. In this case each vector is a row of the matrix:

```
type matrix=array[1..height] of vector
```

In this way, a matrix can be multiplied by a vector using the *innerproduct* function:

```
procedure matbyvector(var a:matrix; var x,y:vector);

  {Form the product y:=Ax}

  var row,col:integer;

  begin
    for row:=1 to height do
      y[row]:=innerproduct(a[row],x);
  end;
```

Exercise Write a procedure to compute the product of two matrices, itself a matrix.

$$c_{mn} = \sum_{k=1}^{r} a_{mk} b_{kn}$$

Here, a is an m by r matrix, b is r by n and the result c is m by n. If the indices of a, b, and c do not relate to each other in this way, then the product is impossible.

6 Conformant parameters with several subscripts

Conformant array parameters are not available in all implementations of Pascal, but if they are, you can match up an actual parameter to a conformant parameter scheme in a **procedure** or **function** declaration. As always, the actual and formal parameters have to correspond exactly in type. However, because an array may be an array of arrays there are a number of arrangements possible. Suppose you have defined

```
var a:array[1..4,1..3] of real;
```

then the array a could be passed to a procedure by writing

```
usesit(a)
```

and defining the formal parameters of *usesit* like this:

```
procedure usesit
  (var ray:array[mini..maxi:integer; minj..maxj:integer]
    of real);
```

Notice the confusing and inconsistent use by Pascal of the semicolon to separate the two indices. You could have this equivalent:

```
procedure usesit
  (var ray:array[mini..maxi:integer]
    of array[minj..maxj:integer] of real);
```

In both these cases, the values of the bounds *mini*, *maxi*, *minj* and *maxj* are available to be used in expressions throughout the procedure.

However, if you had defined an **array** type such as

```
type bigarray=array[1..4,1..3] of real;
var a:bigarray;
```

then you cannot use a as a conformant array parameter.

You could have

```
type vector=array[1..3] of real;
var a:array[1..4] of vector;
```

to use

```
usesit(a)
```

to activate a procedure

```
procedure usesit(var ray:array[min..max:integer] of
                                              vector);
```

You will recall that a conformant array parameter could be either a variable or value parameter, although using value parameters which are arrays is inefficient—it wastes time and memory. In a conformant array scheme, only the final array description in the scheme can be packed. (However the type of this final array could itself be defined as a packed array in a type statement.)

> *Exercise* If conformant array parameters are available to you, implement the inner product of two vectors, the product of a matrix and a vector and also the product of two matrices using them. You must check in your procedures that the index bounds permit the products you are trying to make.

7 Problems

Problem 14.1 To index a book, you could use a program like the one devised in Section 3 of this chapter. You work through your text after it has been set up in type, entering each new item as a string, including the page number, as you find it. Of course it will have to be edited afterwards, but it makes an impossible task just bearable. However, I do not use exactly this program for indexing because bubble sorting is too slow. You could either do the sorting as items are entered by insertion with a binary search, or you could do a quicksort instead of the bubble sort. Investigate these possibilities, in particular implementing both kinds of sorting for 'dynamic strings'.

Problem 14.2 Equations can be solved by 'Cramer's rule' as long as they are not too large. Furthermore it can be specified recursively. Look this up (in any work on linear algebra) and implement it.

Problem 14.3 You can get in trouble with the Gauss elimination method if the 'corner' element *a[corner,corner]* in our program becomes very small at any stage in the elimination process. To minimize this danger, the largest available coefficient below and beyond the corner should be switched into the corner and this process is called *pivotal condensation*. You can interchange two rows of the array to do this without disturbing the solution, but if you switch any columns, you change the order of the answer and have to remember how to put it back at the end. Do it.

Fifteen
About Types

1 Postscript and prelude

We have now completed a 'Crash Course in Pascal' as far as the procedural aspects of the language are concerned, and the remaining chapters are intended to introduce the rest of the language. So far we have covered how things are done, but we have only scratched the surface concerning items that things are done to—the data structures of Pascal. Although this is an important (and innovative) aspect of the language, it is also somewhat deep and cannot be dealt with fully in a crash course. In these last few chapters we also crash through the data structuring facilities of Pascal. Although there is actually more here than in many introductory courses (and nothing has been left out), I recommend a more advanced study if you are ever to use them seriously.

2 Simple types summarized

In Pascal, there are simple types, structured types, and the special pointer type.

The simple types refer to items which are each a single object. Simple types are:

real	(Chapter 3. An integer value may always be substituted for a real.)
integer	(Chapter 4)
boolean	(Chapter 5)
char	(Chapter 13)
subranges of the above	(Section 3 of this chapter)
enumerated types that you create yourself	(Section 4 of this chapter)

Items of the simple types *real*, *integer*, and *char* can be read or written using normal input and output devices—your terminal in most cases. Boolean items can be written but not read. All types which can be written can be given a *fieldwidth* specification in the activation of the procedures *write* or *writeln*. Only the *real* type can be given a *decimalplaces* specification:

$$write(item{:}fieldwidth{:}decimalplaces, \ldots)$$

All the simple types except *real* are ordered, and that means they may be used as indices in subscripting arrays, for selection in case structures or as the index of a **for** loop. For any ordered type, the counting functions will work:

succ(*object*)   the next *object* in order (successor)

pred(*object*)   the previous *object* in order (predecessor)

For example,

succ(3) is 4   pred('Q') is 'P'

succ(false) is *true*   but succ(true) is an error

For assignment of simple types:

variable:=*value*

the *value* must be of the same type as the *variable*, or in the case of a subrange (discussed in the next section), the *value* should lie in the permitted range for the *variable* and be of the correct type. An integer value may be assigned to a real variable.

For comparison of simple types:

value   *relational operator*   *value*

the *value*s must be of the same simple type. An integer value can be compared to a real value.

3 The structured types

Structured types are made up from items of simple type combined into data structures in either packed or unpacked form. The structured types are:

arrays   (Chapters 12, 14)

strings   (*text*, or **packed arrays of** *char*, Chapter 13)

sets   (this chapter)

records   (Chapter 16)

files, including *text* which is a **file of** *char*   (Chapter 17)

Packing of simple types within structures is intended if possible to make them occupy less space in the memory of a computer, and how it is done (if at all) depends on the implementation on your computer. You cannot pass an item from within a packed structure as a **var** parameter to a procedure or function, although the *read* and *readln* procedures are exempt from this rule. Operations on packed data are likely to be slower than on unpacked data. In a conformant array parameter scheme, only the last array can be packed.

Packing is specified for a structure by using the keyword **packed** before the structured type specification in either a **type** or **var** declaration, for example:

```
bytelist:packed array[1..127] of byte;
```

Pascal provides standard procedures for packing and unpacking of values between array variables which are packed and unpacked versions using the same simple type here called *sametype*.

> pack(uncrunched,offset,crunched)

where

> *uncrunched* = the name of a variable which is **array**[*min..max*] **of** *sametype*;
> *crunched* = the name of a **packed array**[*small..large*] **of** *sametype*;

As long as *max − min >= large − small*, then the information is packed from uncrunched into *crunched*, as if this statement were written instead:

> for i:=small to large do crunched[i]:=uncrunched[i−min+offset]

(the *offset* must be chosen to give legal subscripts).

Similarly,

> unpack(crunched,uncrunched,offset)

does

> for i:=small to large do uncrunched[i−min+offset]:=crunched[i]

You may find it easier just to write out the **for** loop when you need it, rather than looking up the order of the parameters for *pack* and *unpack*, because nobody can ever remember these!

Structured types (except the **file** type or structures containing the **file** type) can be used in assignment statements provided they are described by the same type identifier. The implications of this were described in relation to arrays. String types can be assigned if they are the same length.

Among the structured types, only strings of the same length can be compared using relational operators. However, some of the relational operators have special meaning when used with sets, as described later in this chapter.

Strings are also the only structured type which can be written on the standard output file using *write* or *writeln*. The standard output file is a text file, as discussed in Chapter 17, where you will see that structured types can be written to other files of the appropriate type.

You may not create a function whose result is a structured type in standard Pascal. This restriction includes strings, although many extensions to Pascal will allow a string function.

The pointer type, which is the subject of Chapter 18, is very special. Items which are declared in the **var** declarations of Pascal programs are 'static' objects. Pascal also uses dynamic objects which are created (or disposed of) by a program when it is running. The **pointer** type is used to refer to dynamic variables; indeed it is the only way to refer to them. Conversely, a pointer cannot refer to a static object.

4 Subranges

You can create a simple type which is a subrange of an ordered type, i.e. any simple type except *real*. These are quite useful when grouped into sets, as we will see later in this chapter.

Example To create a subrange type called *byte*, based on integers with allowed values in the range from 0 to 255, put

```
type byte=0..255;
```

and then some variables can be used of type *byte*:

```
var thisone:byte;
```

You could just as easily put:

```
var thisone:0..255;
```

but then the variable *thisone* could not be passed to a procedure or function as a variable parameter. This is the same as the array passing problem described earlier. The same type identifier must be used, in this case *byte*, to describe the variable passed and the formal parameter of the procedure. Here is a procedure which shows the printable character that goes with a particular value in the range of *byte*. It is assumed that the character range corresponds to the ASCII code. There are three cases:

range 0 to 31   an ASCII code but not printable

range 32 to 127 a printable ASCII character

range 128 to 255 not an ASCII code

Notice that *byte* is a subrange of the type *integer*, and can be written because values of type *integer* can be passed to *write* or *writeln* (and can be used with *read* or *readln*).

```
program ascode;

   {Demonstrate the use of a subrange type called byte}

   type byte=0..255;

   var test:byte;

   procedure showcode(code:byte);

      {Display the printable ASCII character
           that corresponds to code}

      begin
        writeln;
        write('The code ',code:3);
```

```
            if code<32 then
              writeln(' is ASCII but not printable')
              else if code<128 then
                writeln(' is the ASCII character''',
                  chr(code),'''')
                else if code>127 then
                  write(' is not an ASCII character')
        end;

    {Main program to try this}

    begin
      writeln;
      write('Enter a byte in the range Ø-255 .. ');
      readln(test);
      showcode(test)
    end.
```

You can assign a value from one subrange type to another, if the simple type they are based on is the same, but an execution error will arise if the actual value is out of the variable's range. For example, using

```
type bigger='h'..'z';
smaller='a'..'r';
var last:bigger;
first:smaller;
```

You can have any of these statements, but some could fail when the program is run:

```
last:='m';

first:='e';

first:=last; {Will fail unless last is
                in the range 'h'..'r'}

last:=first; {will fail unless first is
                in the range 'h'..'r'}
```

Subrange values can be used in comparisons as long as the simple values they are based on are of the same type as the other value in the comparison, and recall that an integer value can be compared to a real value. This comparison is allowed whether or not the values of *first* and *last* happen to lie in their common range 'h'..'s':

```
if last<first then writeln('The last shall be first');
```

Because a subrange is an ordered type, it may be used with the *succ* and *pred* functions, and subrange variables may be used as indices if the range is appropriate. This means they can be subscripts of arrays, **case** selectors, and indices in **for** loops, provided that they are defined locally.

5 Enumerated types

An enumerated type is an ordered simple type that you create yourself by giving names to values which are expected, in their desired order. For example, you can say a *rainbow* by putting a list of identifiers in round brackets:

```
type rainbow=(red,orange,yellow,green,blue,violet);
```

in which case the type *rainbow* has the six values stated. *Ord*(*red*) is 0 and the others follow on. *Ord*(*orange*) is 1, and orange is succ(*red*).

Variables of type *rainbow* can be created:

```
var palette:rainbow;
```

You can use an enumerated type to index an array, declared for example as

```
var paintbox:array[red..violet] of integer;
```

and used as a subscript:

```
array[violet]:=34;
```

A variable of enumerated type can also serve as a **case** selector, or the index of a **for** loop. You can assign or compare items of type *rainbow*, and pass them as parameters to preceedures or functions. Unfortunately you cannot *read* or *write* an enumerated type using your normal input/output device. The value *red* is not the string 'red', it is just plain *red*. You can, however, write *ord*(*red*) which is 0, and you could display strings for values of type *rainbow* by making an appropriate procedure. This is seen in the example which follows.

> *Example* Here the use of an enumerated type which represents the months of the year is shown. You can enter a month number and have the actual month displayed. There are other ways of doing this, but the example illustrates one little problem with enumerated types. For the type *char*, the function
>
> > *chr*(*integer value*)
>
> is the opposite of the function
>
> > *ord*(*char value*)

Although *ord* is available for enumerated types, there is no opposite to it for enumerated types, so this little program shows how to make one. *Unord*(*integer*) is the opposite of *ord*(*month*). Another way of doing this with variant record types is shown in Chapter 16.

```
program months;

   {Demonstrate conversions of items of enumerated type}

   {An integer is converted to a month, and the month is
     displayed}

   type
     month=(jan,feb,mar,apr,may,jun,
       jul,aug,sept,oct,nov,dec);
     monthnumber=1..12;

   var testmonth:month;

   procedure showmonth(thismonth:month);

     begin
       writeln;
       write('The month is ');
       case thismonth of
         jan:writeln('January');
         feb:writeln('February');
         mar:writeln('March');
         apr:writeln('April');
         may:writeln('May');
         jun:writeln('June');
         jul:writeln('July');
         aug:writeln('August');
         sept:writeln('September');
         oct:writeln('October');
         nov:writeln('November');
         dec:writeln('December');
       end;
       writeln
     end;

   function unord(imonth:monthnumber):month;

     {Convert integer order to month type}

     var makeamonth:month;
         index:monthnumber;

     begin
       makeamonth:=jan;
       for index:=2 to imonth do
         makeamonth:=succ(makeamonth);
       unord:=makeamonth
     end;
```

```
procedure getmonth(var thismonth:month);

  var imonth:monthnumber;

  begin
    writeln;
    write('Enter the number 1..12 of a month .. ');
    readln(imonth);
    thismonth:=unord(imonth)
  end;

{Main program}

begin
  repeat
    getmonth(testmonth);
    showmonth(testmonth)
  until false
end.
```

You can have subranges of enumerated types, for example with the type *month*:

```
type month=(jan,feb,mar,apr,may,jun,
   jul,aug,sept,oct,nov,dec);
```

you can create subranges like these within the same **type** declaration, or in the **type** declaration of a contained block:

```
firsthalf=jan..jun;
secondhalf=jul..dec;
```

6 Sets

The **set** is a structured type which allows us to form and manipulate collections of values of the same simple ordered type (not *real*). The set concept is a particularly convenient way of discovering whether a particular value falls within the collection. With sets, there are special operators for forming collections, and special relational operators for testing them.

A **set** is declared as

> **set of** *ordered type*

Very often, the type collected into a **set** will be a subrange, as in

```
type lower='a'..'z';
     lowercase=set of lower;
```

Here the type *lower* is a subrange of *char*. A variable of type *lower* could therefore have a value which is any of these letters. The type *lowercase* is a set of values, which could include any of the letters from the subrange *lower*. A variable of type *lowercase* would be used to indicate which letters are currently members of the set. This is the basic concept—a set variable is a list of possible values, unlike an array which is a list of actual values.

A set can be formed directly from a subrange, as in

```
type digits=set of 0..9;
```

An enumerated type can be collected similarly, for example:

```
type months=(jan,feb,mar,apr,may,jun,
   jul,aug,sept,oct,nov,dec);
season=set of months;
```

A particular implementation of Pascal may have a restriction on the number of values in a set. You are certain to be able to have

```
set of boolean
```

and probably

```
set of char
```

You may not be allowed

```
set of integer
```

because of the large number of values it contains.

Set variables are used to manipulate collections of values. For the type *season*, defined above, you could have

```
var spring,summer,autumn,winter:season;
```

The values that we assign to these collections indicate the values or range of values that they contain. A set variable can have assigned to it a list of set elements given in square brackets. You could make this assignment:

```
winter:=[dec,jan,feb]
```

Where the collected elements are in order, you can use a range construction:

```
spring:=[mar..may]
```

```
summer:=[jun..aug];
```

```
autumn:=[sept..nov];
```

You can also have a null set. If nothing is a set variable, then put:

```
nothing:=[]
```

The operations on sets allow us to combine or exclude values. The available ones are:

+   union   (all the values that occur in either set)
*   intersection (only the values that occur in both sets)
−   difference

Examples Using the *months* and *seasons* we could define some additional variables:

```
var niceones,nastyones:season;
```

and say

```
niceones:=spring+summer;
nastyones:=[jan..dec]-niceones ;
```

The relational operators that are available for sets are very useful. They include some of the same symbols as with other types, but with different meanings in some cases:

value **in** *set variable*
   The *value* must be of the simple type that makes up the set. The result is *true* if the value is in the set, *false* if not.

set value = *set value*
   True if the sets contain exactly the same values currently. *False* otherwise.

set value <> *set value*
   True if the sets do not contain exactly the same values. *False* otherwise.

set value <= *set value*
   True if the left *set value* is contained within the right *set value*.

set value >= *set value*
   True if the right *set value* is contained within the left *set value*.

Example We can write a simple program to select our telephone directory. In London, the huge directory is divided into four books containing A−D, E−K, L−R and S−Z. This program tells you which book to use. Notice that the upper and lower case are included.

```
program london;

   {Using set operands, tells you which of
    the London telephone directories to reach for}

   type letters=set of char;

   var   atod,etok,ltor,stoz,alphabet:letters;
         testch:char;
```

```
begin
  atod:=['a'..'d']+['A'..'D'];
  etok:=['e'..'k']+['E'..'K'];
  ltor:=['l'..'r']+['L'..'R'];
  stoz:=['s'..'z']+['S'..'Z'];
  alphabet:=atod+etok+ltor+stoz;
  writeln;
  write('Enter a letter for directory advice .. ');
  readln(testch); writeln;
  if testch in alphabet then
    begin
      write('Use the ');
      if testch in atod then write('A to D ')
        else if testch in etok then write('E to K ')
          else if testch in ltor then write('L to R ')
            else if testch in stoz then write('S to Z ')
    end
  else writeln('That is not in any directory.');
end.
```

7 Problems

Problem 15.1 If you throw several dice simultaneously, the outcome is the sum of the spots facing upwards, a number from 2 to 12 if two are used, which could clearly be represented by a subrange of integers. In a game certain outcomes are winners (7 or 11 or a repeat of your first throw) others are losers (2) and others allow you to throw again. Using sets to describe the winners, losers and try-againers, develop a program to throw dice for you and report the state of the game as it proceeds. The random numbers from Chapter 11 are needed for the dice throwing.

Problem 15.2 The program which you wrote in Problem 12.2 used an array of integers which you sieved for prime numbers. How many primes would your computer allow you to find this way? It could as easily used a set of integers, from which you remove the multiples of all the primes in exactly the same way, but using set operations. Do this. You will find that although the idea works well, you will be restricted to some fairly small subrange of integers as members of the set. Now simulate the set with a packed array of boolean values, in which the index corresponds to an integer, and the value indicates membership or not of the set. How many primes can you get that way? The concept of a set remains extremely valuable, even if you have to simulate it in reality.

Sixteen

Records

1 Defining records

The structured types that we have studied so far are the **set** and the **array**. Both are collections of items which are all of the same type. It is often useful to form a structure from a collection of objects of different types, and this is what a **record** does.

A **record** is a type, and therefore can either be declared as a type identifier or given directly in the **var** declaration. The advantage of using a type identifier is, as always, that items of that type can be assigned and passed as parameters to procedures and functions.

> *Example* Here is (perhaps) another approach to the problem of dynamic strings in Pascal. We define a *strang* to be a record which contains both an integer *count* telling us the string length, and an array of characters. We do not need to sacrifice a filler character using this scheme, because we always know how many characters in the string are occupied:

```
type strang=record
                count:integer;
                symbols:packed array[1..132] of char
            end;
```

There is no reason not to have an array of records (or an array of sets for that matter):

```
paragraph=array[1..2Ø] of strang;
```

In general, to define a record, put as the **type** declaration

> **type** *identifier*=**record**
>   *field name,field name,field name:type;*
>   *field name,field name,field name:type;*
>   :
>   *field name,field name, field name: type*
> **end**;

The list of *field names* spells out the structure of the record and gives the type of each *field*. The scope of each *field name* is the innermost record it is defined in, meaning that the same names could be used for other variables or other structures. This would, however, be poor form as it can only make a program confusing.

2 Using Records

To use a record, a variable is created which is a **record** type, and then the record or its fields can be manipulated. If the record has been given a type identifier, then you can say

variable:=*value*

for one such *variable*. In practice, the only possible *value* is the name of another record since expressions of structured type do not exist. An individual field can be accessed by giving

record name . field name

which then behaves like a variable of the type of the named field, as for example

instrang.count:=∅

if *instrang* is a record variable, and *count* is a field inside it of either real or integer type.

Example Here are some procedures to manipulate this new kind of dynamic string, which is a record type defined at the beginning of the program:

```
program dynastrang;
   {Demonstrates how variable length strings can
       be achieved using the record type strang.}

   const stringmax=132;

   type strang=record
      count:integer;
      symbols:packed array[1..stringmax] of char
   end;

   var one,two,three:strang;

   procedure readastr(var instr:strang);

   {Ask the user to enter a dynamic string}

   var i:integer;

   begin
     writeln;
     writeln('Enter any string .. ');
     i:=∅;
     while (not eoln) and (i<stringmax) do
       begin
         i:=i+1;
         read(instr.symbols[i]);
       end;
     instr.count:=i;
     readln;
   end;
```

```
procedure showastr(var shstr:strang);

  {Display a dynamic string}

  var i:integer;

  begin
    for i:=1 to shstr.count do write(shstr.symbols[i]);
  end;

procedure concat(left,right:strang; var result:strang);

  {Concatenate two dynamic strings and
   Truncate if combined length > stringmax}

  var i,j:integer;

  begin

    {First copy left string}

    for i:=1 to left.count do
      result.symbols[i]:=left.symbols[i];

    {Now right string until out of room}

    i:=left.count;
    j:=∅;
    while (i<stringmax) and (j<right.count) do
      begin
        i:=i+1; j:=j+1;
        result.symbols[i]:=right.symbols[j]
      end;
    result.count:=i;
  end;

{Main program to try this}

begin
  readastr(one); readastr(two);
  concat(one,two,three);
  showastr(three)
end.
```

With complicated records, it can be tedious to write out

  record name . field name

particularly if there are structured types within the record, such as

```
world[index].individuals.people
```

In this situation the **with** statement of Pascal can simplify accessing of records. **With** tells Pascal that we are going to use field identifiers for a list of record variables:

with *recordname, recordname* ... **do** *statement*

Often the *statement* is a compound statement. A *recordname* could specify a particular record variable, such as in this alternative version of *showastr* from the previous example.

```
procedure showastr(var shstr:strang);

  {Display a dynamic string}

  var i:integer;

  begin
    with shstr do for i:=1 to count do write(symbols[i]);
  end;
```

The **with** statement is another structured statement of Pascal. It allows the fields of a record to be accessed directly by their field names. This could take over the names of other Pascal items from the occurrence of a record name to the end of the **with** structure. You could even have one record take over from another. Either of these would be very poor practice. Since a **with** statement could contain another **with** statement, there are alternative ways of referring to nested record structures.

Example The world government keeps a central computer file on its member countries, an array of records. By a resolution of the Insecurity Council, horses and teddy bears also count as citizens. This is the Pascal data structure:

```
const stringmax=132;
      states=20;

type strang=record
       count:integer;
       symbols:packed array[1..stringmax] of char
     end;

     souls=record
       people,horses,teddies:integer
     end;

     country=record
       countryname,headofstate:strang;
       individuals:souls
     end;

     planet=array[1..states] of country;

  var world:planet;
```

We could want to access a record within a record, as in

```
with world[index].country do showastr(headofstate)
```

or the record access could be nested, as in this procedure which prints the worldwide census of citizens:

```
procedure citizens;

  {Do the planetary census of citizens}

  var index, sum, term:integer;

  begin
    sum:=∅;
    for index:=1 to states do
      begin
        with world[index] do
          begin
            write('Constituent state ');
            showastr(countryname);
            writeln;
            with individuals do
              term:=people+horses+teddies;
            writeln('This country has ',term,' citizens');
            sum:=sum+term
          end
      end;
    writeln;
    writeln('The world''s population is ',sum)
  end;
```

The **with** structure has saved us from writing

```
term:=world[index].individuals.people
        + world[index].individuals.horses
          + world[index].individuals.teddies;
```

3 Variant records

In Pascal a record is able to change its composition according to some **case** selector, normally but not always a part of the record. As well as having honest applications, the variant record is often used to cheat on the typing rules of Pascal. A record can have at most one variant part which must be the last field or fields defined in the record, and the different variants must all contain distinct field names. A variant record can contain other variant records.

> *Example* Here a record type *spooks* contains a variant part selected by the type *agency*. A variable called *dossier* is a record which contains within it some fixed fields and a variant selected by the selector field *spy* which is of type *boolean*. Notice that the *spooks* type does not have a selector field, whereas the variant part of *dossier* is selected by *spy*. A field selector such as *spy* is called the *tag field*.

```
{Shows most of the alternatives with
       variant records}

type agency=(kgb,mi5,cia,boa,pig);
     soviets=(factory,farm,bourgois);
     yanks=(republican,democrat,pinko);
     grades=(idiot,fool,blunderer);
     looks=(rare,medium,welldone);
     hardware=(knife,pistol,rifle);
     flower=(tulip,daffodil,lilly);

     spook=record
       case whose:agency of
         kgb:(partymember:boolean;
              parents:soviets;
              kgbgrade:grades);
         mi5:(publicschool,oxbridge,traitor:boolean;
              mi5grade:grades);
         cia:(politics:yanks;
              ciagrade:grades);
         boa,pig:()

     end;

var dossier:record
       description:record
          heightcms,weightkgs:real;
          complexion:looks
       end;
       case boolean of
         true:(weapons:hardware;
               baddie:spook);
         false:(favourite:flower)
    end;
```

In general, a record type or a record variable can declare at most one variant part, which must come at the end of the record. However, the variant record can contain other variant fields previously defined, as the example shows. A variant part is defined by

> **case** *typename* **of**
>   *selection list:*(*field;field; . . . field*);
>   *selection list:*(*field;field; . . . field*);
>   ⋮
>   *selection list:* (*field; field; . . . field*)

or alternatively, using a tag field, write instead

> **case** *tag:typename* **of**

With either choice, the type used for selection must be an ordered type, which means any simple type except *real*. All possible cases must be covered in the *selection list*, which gives the selected values separated by commas. To complete the list, an empty selection () may be used, as shown in the example.

All the fields of the variants must have distinct names. In the example, the parts of the type *grade* have different identifiers even though they probably have the same interpretation to the designer of this data structure.

If you use a tag field, there are two special restrictions. Firstly the tag identifier cannot be passed as a variable parameter to a procedure; this means that a procedure is not allowed to assign a value to the tag without the rest of the record being present. The second restriction applies to the access to a variant record.

To use a value from a variant record, simply access it using its field name in the usual way. Where there is a tag field, you can only access the active variant. Which part is active depends on the current value of the tag:

```
whose:=mi5;
dossier.baddie.traitor:=true
```

is legal, whereas

```
whose:=kgb;
dossier.baddie.politics:=pinko
```

is an error.

Example We have complained about the inability to read and write enumerated types using the normal input and output units. In Chapter 15, a function *unord* turned the integer equivalent of a month into a value of type *month*, but it was inefficient because it had to step through the months using the *succ* function. Here is another way in which we cheat the typing rules of Pascal. We assume that the computer actually stores the subrange 0..11 of integers in the same manner as the *months jan..dec*, which is probably true. We rely on the variants of a record occupying the same actual space in memory. An integer value is read in, and we have set up the subrange 0..11 as the alternative to a *month* in a variant record. I have done it without a tag field, which gives us access to both variants at the same time:

```
function unord(imonth:monthnumber):month;

  {Very cheeky method converts order to month type}

  type monthrange=0..11;

  var makeamonth:record
        case boolean of
          true:(amonth:month);
          false:(animonth:monthrange)
      end;
```

```
begin
  makeamonth.animonth:=imonth-1;
  unord:=makeamonth.amonth
end;
```

Example Here is a really massive cheat. We have an *m* by *n* array of real values and we wish to change its shape to an *n* by *m* array using the same space in memory. That is easy enough using variant records, but we also wish to transpose the contents of the array. This is most easily done using a variant of the array which has only one dimension.

To do it we have to know how Pascal orders the members of an array in the memory of a computer. Suppose there are three arrays which are all variants of the same record:

```
const m=4; n=5; size=19; {Size is m*n-1}
```

```
type shape=(mbyn,nbym,list);
     block=record
       case which:shape of
         mbyn:(ambyn:array[1..m,1..n] of real);
         nbym:(anbym:array[1..n,1..m] of real);
         list:(alist:array[Ø..size] of real);
     end;
```

```
var thisarray:block;
    k,l:integer;
```

The three variants of this array then occupy the same space in the computer's memory, as tabulated here:

m by *n*	*list*	*n* by *m*
ambyn[1,1]	*alist*[0]	*anbym*[1,1]
ambyn[1,2]	*alist*[1]	*anbym*[1,2]
ambyn[1,3]	*alist*[2]	*anbym*[1,3]
ambyn[1,4]	*alist*[3]	*anbym*[1,4]
ambyn[1,5]	*alist*[4]	*anbym*[2,1]
ambyn[2,1]	*alist*[5]	*anbym*[2,2]
ambyn[2,2]	*alist*[6]	*anbym*[2,3]
.	.	.
.	.	.
.	.	.
ambyn[4,5]	*alist*[19]	*anbym*[5,4]

In general, in the *mbyn* case *ambyn*[*i,j*] is stored in the same place as *alist*[*j*−1+(*i*−1)*n*]. In the *nbym* case, *anbym*[*j,i*] is stored with *alist*[*i*−1+(*j*−1)*m*]. To transpose the array, we have to move the value at [*j*−1+(*i*−1)*n*] to [*i*−1+(*j*−1)*m*] for all *i,j* combinations. The rule telling us where to move a particular index of *alist* is worked out by this function:

```
function rule(now:integer):integer;

   {Apply the cyclic permutation rule to get
    the next position after now in the cycle}

   var i,j:integer;

   begin
     {First undo now into i,j subscripts}
     i:=(now) div n;
     j:=(now) mod n;
     {Make the next value from j,i subscript}
     rule:=i+j*m
   end;
```

Now the complications set in. If *m* and *n* are not the same, [*i,j*] does not exchange with [*j,i*]. The series of moves from a particular starting place form a cyclic permutation which eventually returns to the starting place. You cannot predict in general how many of these cycles there are. Usually there are several. If we are dealing with a 4x5 array, there are two of them:

list[0]   stays put (it always does)
list[1] ☞ [4] ☞ [16] ☞ [7] ☞ [9] ☞ [17] ☞ [11] ☞ [6] ☞ [5] ☞ [1]
list[2]   starts another cycle which includes the rest, except
list[19]   which stays put

We could stop after the cycle on *list*[2] in the 4x5 case, but in general we have to keep searching for new cycles. We can spot an old cycle because it returns to an index before the starting place, which must have been done earlier. Here is a procedure which looks forward by recursion until it finds the end of a cycle, or dicovers that it has been done before. Then, as the recursion unwinds, the necessary moves are made. A very nice and useful application of recursion:

```
procedure cycle(start,now:integer; var doit:boolean);
   var next:integer;
       save:real;

   begin

     {First work through the cycle until either the
      end is reached or it has been done before}

     next:=rule(now);
     write(' to ',next:3);
     if next<start then
       begin
         writeln(' .. Don''t do this one.');
         doit:=false
       end
     else if next>start then cycle(start,next,doit)
       else doit:=true;
```

```
                  {If this is a new cycle, switch two values}

              if (doit) and (next<> start) then
                with thisarray do
                  begin
                    save:=alist[now];
                    alist[now]:=alist[next];
                    alist[next]:=save
                  end;
      end;
```

Here is the rest of the program, a procedure to transpose which does all the possible cycles, and a main program to try it out. I have kept some tracing statements in the program so you can follow it around. Notice how the different variants of this array are selected by the tag field *which*. It is read in as an *mbyn*, transposed as a *list*, and passed back as an *nbym*:

```
procedure transpose;

    {Obtain the transpose of thisarray by cyclic permutation}

    var index:integer;
        didit:boolean;

    begin
      with thisarray do
        begin
          which:=list;
          for index:=1 to size-1 do
            begin
              writeln;
              write('Cycle on ',index:3);
              cycle(index,index,didit);
            end;
          which:=nbym
        end
    end;

    {Main program to try this out}

    begin
      with thisarray do
        begin
          which:=mbyn;
          writeln;
          writeln('Enter a matrix 4 rows by 5 columns');
          for k:=1 to 4 do
            for l:=1 to 5 do
              read(ambyn[k,l]);
          writeln; writeln;
          transpose;
```

```
      writeln('The transpose of this is ..');
      writeln;
      for k:=1 to 5 do
        begin
          for l:=1 to 4 do
            write(anbym[k,l]);
          writeln;
        end
  end
end.
```

4 Problems

Problem 16.1 Design a record structure which describes the bookings on a particular airline flight. A seat may be free or empty, and in one of several sections of the aircraft. Remember the non-smokers and the early birds who want window seats, for example. Personal and other useful details of the passenger are also required. For example are they vegetarians, or can they either deliver the pilot's baby or fly the plane themselves? Develop a program which will take bookings for the flight.

Seventeen
Files

1 Defining files—a structured type

Conceptually a file is a structure containing a sequence of items which are all of the same type. Physically a file almost certainly is connected to some external device—such as your keyboard, screen or disk storage. We use the data in a file sequentially, by working through it one item at a time from the beginning, mainly using the *read, readln, write* and *writeln* procedures.

As with other types, a file variable is created by a **var** declaration, with its type being given either in a **type** declaration, or directly as part of the **var** declaration. You can have a file of any type which does not itself contain a file. For example, we can have

```
type junk=(bottles,cans,paper,rottingvegetables);
     junkfile=file of junk;
var receptacle:junkfile;
```

or, alternatively,

```
var picturefile:file of array[1..512,1..512] of 0..255;
```

When we declare a variable which is a file, a 'buffer' is created for us, and we send and receive information through the buffer, which is our program's window onto the file. We discuss direct use of the buffer variable to manipulate the file at the end of Chapter 18.

One type of file is declared for us in advance. This is the type *text*, which is a **file of** *char* including an end of line symbol.

```
type text=file of char;    {including end of line}
```

Two actual file variables are also predeclared which are both of type *text*. These are called *input* and *output*, and we have used them extensively already. The file *input* is your standard device for communicating with Pascal, which is probably a keyboard. The file *output* is your screen or printer.

If you are going to use any external files other than *input* and *output*, you may or may not have to give their names in the **program** statement. This depends on your computer system.

2 Using input and output—the interactive file dilemma

You can assume that the following declarations have been made for you in every Pascal program:

```
type text=file of char; {plus an end of line code}
var input,output:text;
```

We already know of the standard procedures *write, writeln, read* and *readln* which operate on the *input* and *output* files.

> *write(list)*

displays the *list* of items on the file *output*. The items in the *list* can only have simple types that can be displayed as text, separated by commas. The allowed items are of type *real, integer, boolean, char* or character strings, either constants or variables as discussed in Chapter 13. The procedure *writeln* is the same, except that a new line is begun after all the items in the *list* have been written. *Writeln* is only available for files of text. You can control the field width of any of these items, and the number of decimal places used with reals, as was described in Chapters 3 and 4.

Similarly, the procedures *read* and *readln* accept information in the form of text from the file *input*. *Readln* is only available for files of text.

> *read(variables)*

The list of *variables*, separated by commas, can be *real, integer* or *char* but might refer to items within a structured type. The values provided from the input file must be characters which represent values of the correct type, separated by spaces or newlines. The *read* procedure is exempt from the rule which forbids you to pass items from a packed structure as **var** parameters. This allows you to read characters into strings—one at a time.

You can now see that the types of data allowed in the files *input* and *output* are restricted because these are *text* files. We also know from Chapter 13 of the boolean *eoln* function and the problems it causes for an interactive input file. The function *eoln* should become *true* when there are no more characters on a line. If you try to read another one, you get a blank, and *eoln* is then *false* because you are about to move into the next line.

It is impossible for an interactive file to comply with the Pascal standard, because in the case of an empty input line, *eoln* would have to be *true* before the line is typed! Different Pascal implementations cope with this problem in different ways. In one that I know, the standard is followed except that you cannot distinguish an empty line from a line containing exactly one blank. In both cases you get a space with *eoln=true* (which is incorrect for the empty line) followed by a space with *eoln=false* (which is correct). In another system that I know, the *eoln* occurs with the space between lines rather than with the last actual character. This does not follow the Pascal standard, but is probably the way Pascal ought to have been defined in the first place!

> *Example* The procedure *getname* asks the user for the name of a file to process and places it in the variable parameter *thisname*. The type *filename* is a character string, such as

```
filename=packed array[1..14] of char;
```

This version assumes that *eoln* conforms to the Pascal standard. The name is filled with the ASCII character *chr*(0), which is the null character.

```
program getname1;

    type filename=packed array[1..14] of char;

    var testname:filename;
        i:1..14;

    procedure getaname(var thisname:filename);

      {Get the user's file name}

      var index:1..15;
          ch:char;

      begin
        write('Enter the name of your file .. ');
        index:=1;
        repeat
          read(ch);
          thisname[index]:=ch;
          index:=index+1
        until eoln or(index>14);

        {Pad it out with nulls}

        for index:=index to 14 do thisname[index]:=chr(∅);
      end;

    {Test it}

    begin
      getaname(testname);
      writeln;
      for i:=1 to 14 do write(testname[i])
    end.
```

3 Other text files

Very often we wish to process a file that is not *input* or *output*, but which is some other file stored on an external device such as a magnetic disk. To process a file like this, simply declare a suitable file variable. The standard Pascal procedures *reset* and *rewrite* are then used to gain access to the files:

reset(filename)

>to obtain access to the beginning of the file *filename* so that we can *read* from it. You can assume that *reset(input)* is done for you.

rewrite(filename)

>to obtain access to the beginning of the file *filename* so that we can *write* to it. You can assume that *rewrite(output)* is done for you.

As with *input* and *output*, reading or writing are sequential from the beginning of the file. You cannot have access to the same file for reading and writing at the same time.

We can then say

>*write(filename,list)*
>>{*write(list)* is the same as *write(output,list)*}

>*writeln(filename,list)*   is only available for files of *text*.
>>{*writeln(list)* is the same as *writeln(output,list)*}

>*read(filename,list)*
>>{*read(list)* is the same as *read(input,list)*}

>*readln(filename,list)*   is only available for files of *text*.
>>{*readln(list)* is the same as *readln(input,list)*}

For text files only, the procedure *page* causes output to jump to a new page if the file is on a suitable device.

>*page*   moves to a new page on the file *output*.

>*page(filename)*   moves to a new page on the file *filename*.

For a text file which we are reading, we have an end of line indicator which we can test with

>*eoln(filename)*
>>{*eoln* with no *filename* is the same as *eoln(input)*}

We also have

>*eof(filename)*

which is *true* if there is no more information in a file which we are reading, *false* otherwise. It means 'end of file'. Although *eof* is the same as *eof(input)*, it shoulds never be *true* if the input file is an interactive one, such as your keyboard.

Exactly how the connection is achieved between the *filename* in your Pascal program and the physical file in your computer system is not specified by the Pascal standard. In some systems, your filename has to be given in the **program** heading:

```
program yucc(inputfile,outputfile);
```

In others, any file variable name can be converted to any actual file name in the computer system through non-standard extra parameters of *reset* and *rewrite*. For example, on one computer I use:

> *reset(filevariable,namestring,extensionstring)*

and

> *rewrite(filevariable, namestring,extensionstring)*

where

> *filevariable* is the file variable used to access the file through *read* and *write* in the Pascal program.

> *namestring* is a character string constant or variable which gives the actual name in the computer's filing system.

> *extensionstring* is an optional string constant or variable which gives an extension to the file name.

This is very convenient if your computer does it that way. The extension facility allows different versions or variations on a file of the same name.

> *Example* Some students created programs (not in Pascal) using lower case letters, not realizing that the language they were using insisted on capital letters only. I quickly (well, fairly quickly) wrote this program to save them the trouble of retyping or drastically editing their programs. Their file names may or may not have an extension which begins with '.', for example PROG.TXT. The new file that is created has the same name, but its extension (if any) is removed and replaced by '.UCC', for example PROG.UCC, to indicate a file that has been upper case converted. You will notice the non-standard procedure

> *close(filevariable)*

which is necessary on that particular computer to make the result permanent.

```
program yucc;   {Your Upper Case Converter}

   {Takes an input text file named by the user and
      converts all the lower case letters to upper case}

   var infile:text;
       outfile:text;
       ch:char;
       i,j:integer;
       name:packed array[1..14] of char;

   {Main program}

   begin
     writeln;
     write('Welcome to YUCC, your friendly ');
     writeln('conversion to upper case.');
```

{Get the user's file name}

```
write('Enter file name with extension ... ');
i:=1;
repeat
  read(ch);
  name[i]:=ch;
  i:=i+1
until eoln or (i>14);
```

{Pad with nulls and open the file}

```
for i:=i to 14 do name[i]:=chr(∅);
reset(infile,name);        {Nonstandard form of reset}
writeln('We are converting ',name);
writeln;
```

{Rip the extension off the name}

```
i:=∅;
repeat
  i:=i+1
until (name[i]='.') or (i=14);
for i:=i to 14 do name[i]:=chr(∅);
```

{Open the output file with the extension .UCC}

```
rewrite(outfile,name,'.UCC');   {Nonstandard form
                                    of rewrite}
```

{Now do the conversion to upper case}

```
repeat
  read(infile,ch);
  if ch in ['a'..'z'] then

    {Convert ch to upper case}

    ch:=chr(ord('A')+(ord(ch)-ord('a')));
  write(outfile,ch);
  write(ch);

  {Check here for one or more ends of line}

  while eoln(infile) and not eof(infile) do
    begin
      writeln(outfile);
      writeln;
      read(infile,ch)
    end
until eof(infile);
```

```
                {All finished}

      writeln(outfile);
      writeln;
      close(outfile);                    {Not a standard procedure}
      writeln('All finished now');
      writeln('The name of your YUCCed file is ',name,'.UCC');
      writeln
   end.
```

Exercise Find out how to obtain access to named files in your computer system, and make the program *yucc* work for you. It is important to discover how file access from within a Pascal program is implemented on your computer, because all of them are different. Note that the program has no procedures, an indication of the haste with which it was written. Improve it.

4 Files of other types

You can have a file of any type—simple or structured, except that a file type may not contain within it another file type. In this way, any data structure can reside on an external file and be manipulated by a Pascal program. When you use the *read* or *readln* procedures, the data type in the physical file must correspond to the structure of the data type you are trying to read, or terrible errors might occur. (On the other hand, this could be another way of cheating on the typing rules of Pascal.)

Example A digitized photograph is stored on an external file in an array of integers in the subrange 0..127. You could define the types:

```
type gray=0..127;
     picture=array[1..512,1..512] of gray;
     album=file of picture;
     histogram=array[gray] of integer;
```

and the variables:

```
var photo:picture;
    picfile:album;
    hist:histogram;
    i,j:1..512;
    level:gray;
```

and make a histogram of the gray levels that occur in the picture:

```
begin
  reset(picfile);
  read(picfile,photo);
  for level:=0 to 127 do hist[level]:=0;
  for i:=1 to 512 do
```

```
     for j:=1 to 512 do
       begin
         level:=photo[i,j];
         if hist[level]<maxint then
             hist[level]:=hist[level+1]
           else writeln('Histogram overflow')
       end;
    for level:=0 to 127 do write(hist[level]:6)
   end.
```

5 Problems

Problem17.1 Design a record structure for your Christmas card list. Develop a program to read it from an external file, update it, and place it on file again.

Problem 17.2 Using a file of sets, or even a file of packed arrays of boolean, we can sieve for primes beyond the memory capacity of the computer. Sieving for primes was the basis of Problem 12.3 and Problem 15.2. Now see how many primes you can find.

Problem 17.3 Design, implement and test a spelling checker which learns new words by building its own dictionary as it is used. The program reads in the old dictionary, and checks every word in a chosen text file against the dictionary. Every word not found in the dictionary is questioned, and the user indicates whether the new word should be ignored or placed in the dictionary. At the end of the run, the new dictionary is saved. Many sophistications of this basic program are possible, but do it simply, at least to begin with.

Eighteen
Pointers

1 What is a pointer ?

The variables that we have used until now have been static objects, defined in **var** declarations. These are created whenever a procedure or program is activated. We have one and only one version of each object which exists as long as the block containing it is active.

Pointers enable us to have dynamic objects. We can create as many similar objects as we want, when we want them. Objects which are records can be made to point at one another, and so a great variety of data structuring possibilities are made available.

A static object has a name which is established in a **var** declaration. A dynamic object has no name. Instead we have a pointer variable which points at a dynamic object, and this is the purpose of the **pointer** type. Pointers can only be used with dynamic variables, and dynamic variables can only be referred to using pointers—so they are intimately bound together. A pointer itself can be either a static object or a dynamic one. Indeed, the dynamic variable is nearly always a record which contains other pointers. These enable us to create and use a data structure from records that are linked together by pointers.

A pointer type can be declared using the specification $\wedge type\ name$. The declaration

```
type thingpointer=∧thing;
```

creates a **pointer** type called *thingpointer* which we use to point at a *thing*, whatever that is. The symbol $\wedge$ translates as 'points at' in a declaration. We can make static pointer variables:

```
var finger:thingpointer;
    roadsign:∧road;
```

As always, the advantage of using a type identifier like *thingpointer* is that variables of that type can be passed to procedures and can have values assigned to them.

In the above declarations, *finger* is a pointer variable that we can use to point at a *thing*, and *roadsign* can be used to point at a *road*. It is also possible to point a pointer at nothing, by giving it the value *nil*. Initially every pointer is undefined, which is not the same as *nil*. It is a serious error to try to use a pointer which is undefined. We create an object and point the pointer at it with the procedure *new*. For example

```
new(roadsign)
```

will create a *road* and point *roadsign* at it. Then *roadsign* has a value (it points at the *road*), and we can use the *road* itself by writing, for example,

```
roadsign∧
```

which means 'the value pointed at by *roadsign*'.

We can create other *road*s by using the procedure *new*, and we can dispose of a *road* using the procedure *dispose*, for example

```
dispose(roadsign)
```

After we do that, the pointer *roadsign* is undefined and it would be an error to refer to it until it is given a new value. You can also specify which variant of a variant record type that you wish to create, if the variant has tag fields. This can sometimes save space because only enough room is created for the selected variant. However, you cannot later change your mind about which variant you are using:

$$new(pointer,tag1,tag2,...)$$

the items *tag1*, *tag2*, . . ., must be consecutive constants of the correct type and in the correct order to define the variant that you want to create. You can leave out trailing tags to give you access to different variants of fields at the end of the record structure. These constants do not define the actual tag fields in the new record—you have to do that separately. If you have done this, you may not make an assignment to the entire record structure using *pointer*∧, although you can assign individual fields. This form is not often used.

To dispose of a record with its variants specified, you have to use exactly the same list of tag constants to get rid of it:

$$dispose(pointer,tag1,tag2,...)$$

2 Stacks

We can quite easily create a stack of records using pointers. A stack is a list of items which has a variable number of items in it. It could, of course, be an array but we would then have to allocate the maximum expected space to it. By using dynamic records we can create only as much as we need, and release the space again when we are finished.

We place items on the 'top' of a stack, and at any time we can remove the item from the top of the stack. This is a Last In, First Out (LIFO) stack. We need to do only two operations on the stack:

push   place a new item on top of the stack.

pop   recover the item from the stack top, exposing the previous one if any.

Let us implement a stack of *strang*s. A *strang*, you may recall, is a record type that we have used to achieve dynamic strings. To make a stack, we define a *strangstackpointer* as being a pointer to a *strangstack*. Within the *strangstack*, each item must have a *strangstackpointer* to the item below it in the stack, or *nil* at the bottom to show that there are no more. This appears to require the type *strangstack* to be defined before *strangstackpointer* which has to be defined before *strangstack* ! To get around this problem in linking records, the *only* exception to the 'define before use' rule is that the *type name* given as the target of a pointer can be defined later in the **type** declaration. So to make a stack we create these types:

```
program stack;

   {Demonstrates a stack of strangs using the pointer type}

   const stringmax=132;

   type strang=record
         count:integer;
         symbols:packed array[1..stringmax] of char
      end;
   strangstackpointer=∧strangstack;
   strangstack=record
      stackstrang:strang;
      nextstrang:strangstackpointer
   end;
```

You can see how a *strangstackpointer* is defined as a pointer to a *strangstack*. We need a static pointer variable *stacktop* to keep track of the top of our stack:

```
var stacktop:strangstackpointer;

    one:strang;
    i:integer;
```

A *strangstack* which has three active components to it would look like this:

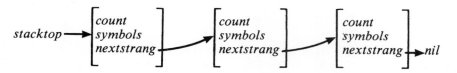

Here is the procedure *pushastrang* to push a *strang* onto the stack. Notice that *thistrang* is a **var** parameter—not because it is necessary, but to save Pascal the time and space involved in making a copy of it when the procedure is activated. Notice also that when the new item is created using *new*, it must have a previous *stacktop* transferred to it. This is how the continuity of the stack is maintained. This is a required feature in any data structure organized as records linked by pointers.

```
   procedure pushastrang(var thistrang:strang);

      {Push thistrang onto the stack of strangs}

      var points:strangstackpointer;

   begin
      {Save the last pointer}
      points:=stacktop;
```

```
      new(stacktop);
      {Put in the strang}
      stacktop∧.stackstrang:=thistrang;
      {Point at the previous entry}
      stacktop∧.nextstrang:=points
   end;
```

Similarly, we can pop an item from the stack using the procedure *popastrang*. In this case the pointer to the following item in the stack is transferred to *stacktop*, by saving it before the stack item is disposed of:

```
   procedure popastrang(var thistrang:strang);

   {Pop a strang out of the stack}

   var points:strangstackpointer;

   {It might be empty}

   begin
     if stacktop<>nil then
       begin
         {Not empty, so pop it out}
         thistrang:=stacktop∧.stackstrang;
         {Save pointer to next stack item}
         points:=stacktop∧.nextstrang;
         {Dispose of top item on stack}
         dispose(stacktop);
         {And point to the new old top}
         stacktop:=points
       end
     else writeln('Nothing there, boyo!');
   end;
```

This main program tests the stack of *strangs*. Note that to make it work correctly, the pointer *stacktop* is first given the value *nil*. The procedures *readastr* and *showastr* come from Chapter 16.

```
   {Main program to try this}

   begin
     stacktop:=nil;
     for i:=1 to 3 do
       begin
         readastr(one); pushastrang(one)
       end;
     for i:=1 to 4 do
       begin
         popastrang(one);
         showastr(one)
       end
   end.
```

3 The queue

With the stack, we have seen how pointers are used in the creation of records and also in linking records together. The stack is a Last In, First Out (LIFO) list of variable length. A queue is a First In, First Out (FIFO) list, and indeed is sometimes considered to be another kind of stack. In the queue, we need to know both the front and the back of the queue. Instead of pointing forward, each record has to point back. Here is the Pascal definition of a queue of *strang*s:

```
const stringmax=132;

type strang=record
     count:integer;
     symbols:packed array[1..stringmax] of char
   end;
   strangqueuepointer=∧strangqueue;
   strangqueue=record
     previous:strangqueuepointer;
     queuestrang:strang
   end;
```

This is what it looks like with three *strang*s in the queue:

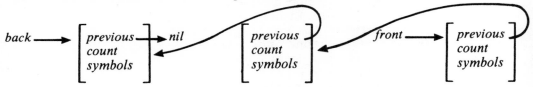

Exercise You implement procedure *join* to add a *strang* to the back of the queue, and *next* to take out the next item from the front of the queue. Consider how each must behave if the queue is empty or becomes empty. Remember that a *nil* pointer is useful, while an undefined pointer is an error.

4 Linked lists

A stack is a list which is linked forward—each record contains a pointer to the next one. A queue is linked backwards. There is a more general case of linked lists in which each record is linked both forwards and backwards. Using *strang*s yet again as records, here is how you might define a linked list with pointers *next* and *previous*:

```
const stringmax=132;

type strang=record
     count:integer;
     symbols:packed array[1..stringmax] of char
   end;
   listpointer=∧stranglist;
   stranglist=record
     previous:listpointer;
```

```
        liststrang:strang;
        next:listpointer
      end;

    var thisone:listpointer;
```

The first item in the list should have *previous* as *nil*, and the last should have the *nil* value for *next*. A list with three items should look like this:

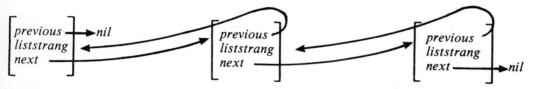

The procedure for inserting a list item has to be written carefully. The new record has to point both ways at the ones surrounding it, and they both have to point at the new record. This procedure inserts a *strang* after the item pointed at by the variable parameter *presentpointer*, which must either point at an actual list item, or have the value *nil* if the list is empty. Notice that it has been carefully written (and tested) to work if the list is empty, if it contains only one item, or if we are at the end of a list.

```
    procedure insertafter(var thistrang:strang;
      var presentpointer:listpointer);

    {Insert thistrang in the list of strangs
       after presentpointer}

    var prevsave,nextsave:listpointer;

    begin

      if presentpointer<>nil then
        begin

          {Save the links to the new record}

          prevsave:=presentpointer;
          nextsave:=presentpointer∧.next
        end
      else
        begin

          {This is the first one}

          prevsave:=nil;
          nextsave:=nil
        end;
```

```
                {Create a new record}

                new(presentpointer);
                presentpointer^.liststrang:=thistrang;

                {Make the links in the new record}

                presentpointer^.previous:=prevsave;
                presentpointer^.next:=nextsave;

                {Make the old records point at this one}

                if prevsave<>nil then prevsave^.next:=presentpointer;
                if nextsave<>nil then
                  nextsave^.previous:=presentpointer
              end;
```

Similar care has to be taken in deleting a list item:

```
        procedure deletelist(var presentpointer:listpointer);

         {Remove a record from the linked list}

         var prevsave,nextsave:listpointer;

         begin

            {Save back pointer and make links
               around the deleted record}

            if presentpointer<>nil then
              begin
                with presentpointer^ do
                  begin
                    prevsave:=previous;
                    nextsave:=next;
                    if previous<>nil then previous^.next:=next;
                    if next<>nil then next^.previous:=previous
                  end;

            {Dispose of old record and point at the one before it
               if any, otherwise the one after, which might be nil}

                dispose(presentpointer);
                if prevsave<>nil then presentpointer:=prevsave
                  else presentpointer:=nextsave
              end
         end;
```

There are a lot of other operations you might want to do on a list. This procedure finds the beginning of a linked list. Its parameter points at any list item, and it works its way to the top, which is detected by a *previous* field being the *nil* pointer.

```
procedure gettop(var presentpointer:listpointer);

    {Find the top of the list}

    begin
      if presentpointer<>nil then
        while presentpointer∧.previous<>nil do
          presentpointer:=presentpointer∧.previous
    end;
```

If you want to display a complete list of *strang*s, do this:

```
procedure printlist(presentpointer:listpointer);

    {Display the entire list}

    var i:integer;

    begin
      gettop(presentpointer);
      writeln;
      while presentpointer<>nil do
        begin
          with presentpointer∧.liststrang do
            for i:=1 to count do write (symbols[i]);
          writeln;
          presentpointer:=presentpointer∧.next
        end
    end;
```

Exercise Write a procedure *insertbefore* which inserts a *strang* before the present pointer. How else could you insert a record before the first one in the list? Write a procedure to position the pointer at the *n*th entry in a list, or the bottom if there are fewer than *n* entries.

5 Trees

The tree structure is very special. In a binary tree, every record can point to a further record on its left and a record on its right. If there are $2n-1$ items in a perfectly balanced tree, then a pointer can be used to search from the root of the tree to any record in at most $n-1$ moves. This is very efficient for searching. A tree with 1023 members can be searched in 9 moves! Look at this simple tree and see:

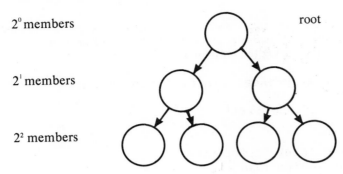

2^0 members   root

2^1 members

2^2 members

We will create—you guessed it—a tree of *strang*s. By limiting the length of a string to 24 symbols, we are going to use a tree structure to make an alphabetical list of all the different words that occur in a file of text, along with how many times each occurs.

Our data structure contains all the structured types of Pascal, but the important one in this example is the *branch* of a tree.

```
program words;

  {Make a word frequency list from a text file}

const stringmax=24;

type strang=record
       count:integer;
       symbols:packed array[1..stringmax] of char
     end;
     branchpointer=∧branch;
     branch=record
       branchstrang:strang;
       frequency:integer;
       left,right:branchpointer
     end;
     charset=set of char;

  var treepointer:branchpointer;
      nextword:strang;
      finished,finder:boolean;
      infile:text;
      wordstarters,wordsymbols:charset;
```

A *branch* in the tree looks like this:

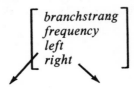

$$\begin{bmatrix} branchstrang \\ frequency \\ left \\ right \end{bmatrix}$$

The main program has the classic *startup*, *doit* and *quit* structure:

```
{The main program}

begin
  startup;
  repeat
    getaword(nextword);
    if not finished then
      begin
        finder:=false;
        addtotree(nextword,treepointer,finder)
      end
  until finished;
  printree(treepointer)
end.
```

The procedure *startup* asks you what text file you want to process, and *resets* it. As with other programs using external files, the exact form of *reset*, and possible file names required in the **program** statement, are dependent on your computer system. *Startup* also defines the sets of characters which are allowed to start a word (any alphabetic one) and those which are allowed to occur in a word (alphabetic, numbers and the apostrophe). We start with a *treepointer* set to *nil*, and the boolean variable *finished* is *false* until the end of the text file is found:

```
procedure startup;

  {Get the user's file name and open input file}

  var ch:char;
      i,j:integer;
      name:packed array[1..14] of char;

  begin
    writeln;
    writeln('This is the word list tree program.');
    writeln;

    {Get the user's file name}

    write('Enter text file name with extension ... ');
    i:=1;
    repeat
      read(ch);
      name[i]:=ch;
      i:=i+1
    until eoln or (i>14);
```

```
{Pad with nulls and open the file}

for i:=i to 14 do name[i]:=chr(Ø);
reset(infile,name);        {Nonstandard form of reset}
writeln;
writeln('We are reading the file ',name);
writeln;

{Initialize the global variables}

treepointer:=nil;
finished:=false;
wordstarters:=['A'..'Z']+['a'..'z'];
wordsymbols:=wordstarters+['Ø'..'9']+['''];

end;
```

The procedure *getaword* retrieves one word from the text file and gives it to us in a *strang* filled with *chr*(0) (in ASCII this is the null character). A word is any sequence of symbols starting with one which is in the set *wordstarters*, and continuing with any number of symbols from the set *wordsymbols* up to the maximum length, 24. To get a word, we simply scan the text file for as many *wordsymbols* as there are. We are not worried by *eoln* because it will always terminate a word, but we must be alert for the end of file *eof(infile)*, which tells us we are finished. Notice that the apostrophe is removed if it is the last symbol and the one before it is not 's'. If you think about it, it is hard to make the rules for word formation fit all the quirks of the English language. What about hyphens? I have settled for a simple but effective rule, but one which is not perfect. Here is *getaword*, which is a nice piece of text processing but nothing to do with tree structures:

```
procedure getaword(var word:strang);

   {Obtain the next word in lower case from the input file}

var gotfirst,gotlast:boolean;
    ch:char;
    num:integer;

begin

   {The next alphabetic character begins the word}

   gotfirst:=false;
   num:=Ø;
   while (not finished) and (gotfirst=false) do
      begin
         read(infile,ch);
         if eof(infile) then finished:=true;
         if ch in wordstarters then gotfirst:=true
      end;
```

```
{Beginning of word has been found}

if not finished then
  begin
    word.symbols[1]:=ch;
    num:=1;

    {Fill strang while searching for end of word}

    gotlast:=false;
    while (not finished) and (gotlast=false) do
      begin
        read(infile,ch);
        if eof(infile) then finished:=true;
        if ch in wordsymbols then
          begin
            num:=num+1;
            if num<=stringmax then
              word.symbols[num]:=ch
          end
        else gotlast:=true
      end;

    {The word has been found. If the
     last  symbol is ' then remove it.}

    if (word.symbols[num]='''') and
      (word.symbols[num-1]<>'s') then num:=num-1;
    word.count:=num;

    {Fill out with nulls}

    for num:=num+1 to stringmax do
      word.symbols[num]:=chr(0);
    lower(word)
  end
end;
```

Before getting into the actual trees, two other procedures are also required. *Showastr* we have had before. *Lower* converts all the letters in the word to lower case:

```
procedure showastr(var shstr:strang);

  {Display a dynamic string}

  var i:integer;

  begin
    for i:=1 to shstr.count do write(shstr.symbols[i]);
  end;
```

```
procedure lower(var word:strang);

{Convert word to lower case}

var i:integer;

begin
  with word do
    for i:=1 to count do
      if symbols[i] in ['A'..'Z'] then
        symbols[i]:=chr(ord('a')+
          (ord(symbols[i])-ord('A')))
end;
```

Now for the tree. I have in fact defined it recursively. We first enter *addtotree* with a *word* to place in alphabetical order in the tree, and with the variable *found* having the value *false* (see the main program). If the tree pointer is *nil* at that point, we are creating the root. Otherwise the *word* is less than, equal to or greater than the *branchstrang* pointed at by *tree*. If equal, we simply increment the frequency counter. Otherwise we have to move left or right down the tree—by calling *addtotree* again, recursively using either the *left* or *right* pointer. Eventually we will find the *word*, or hit a *nil* pointer. So for every word in the textfile, either we create a new branch or we find it already there and increment its frequency:

```
procedure addtotree(word:strang; var tree:branchpointer;
    var found:boolean);

{Search the tree for the word. Increment its frequency
  count if it is there already, otherwise add it and
  set up new links}

begin
  if not found then
    if tree<>nil then
      with tree∧ do
        begin

          {Is word in the present record?}

          if word.symbols=branchstrang.symbols then
            begin
              found:=true;
              frequency:=frequency+1
            end
          else if word.symbols<branchstrang.symbols then
                 addtotree(word,left,found)
               else addtotree(word,right,found)
        end
```

```
        else
          begin

            {Create the new record and link it back}

            new(tree);
            with tree∧ do
              begin
                branchstrang:=word;
                frequency:=1;
                left:=nil;
                right:=nil
              end
          end
    end;
```

Printing the tree is a very pleasing recursion. We work down the tree going to the *left* until we hit a *nil* pointer. As we return from any left branch, we print the current branch, then go to the *right*.

```
    procedure printree(tree:branchpointer);

      {Print the tree from left to right}

    begin
      if tree<>nil then
        begin
          printree(tree∧.left);
          showastr(tree∧.branchstrang);
          writeln(tree∧.frequency:5);
          printree(tree∧.right)
        end
    end;
```

Exercise Write a program which prints a tree in tree form, i.e. print each level before going to the next.

6 Buffer variables—get and put

In describing the procedures *reset* and *rewrite* in Chapter 17, I said that buffer variables were created for the files when *reset* and *rewrite* were used. These are effectively pointers and are not often used directly, so I have left them to the end. You can actually use the buffers of a file directly, along with the special procedures *get* and *put*. In fact *read*, *readln*, *write* and *writeln* are defined in terms of *get* and *put*.

Get is used with input files. The procedure

$$reset(filename)$$

gives access to the file if it exists and creates a buffer variable *filename*∧. You will recognize this as a pointer type, and it always points at the next value in the file. (This is the source of the interactive file dilemma. You should, for example at the very beginning of your program, have access to the character *input*∧, whereas you know by common sense that you do not because it has probably not been entered yet.)

The procedure

> *get(filename)*   or just *get* for the file *input*

moves the *filename*∧ to the next item in the file.

The procedure

> *read(filename,item)*

is the same as

```
begin item:=filename∧; get(filename) end;
```

so that you in fact have access through *filename*∧ to the next item in the file at any time. It can sometimes be useful to read the same item several times; particularly in connection with variant record cheating.

You already know that

> *read(filename,one,two, . . .)*

is the same as

> *read(filename,one)*
> *read(filename,two)*
> .
> .
> .

and that the procedure *readln*, which is only available for text files,

> *readln(filename,items)*

is the same as

> *read(filename,items)*; *readln(filename)*

For a complete description of input in terms of *get*, the only other thing we need is that

> *readln(filename)*

is the same as

```
begin while not eoln get(filename); get(filename) end;
```

Notice that a further *get* is used after *eoln* is *true*. This means that that buffer variable points at the beginning of the next line, unless of course this is the end of file, in which case you are in trouble for not checking it first.

Put works similarly with output files. The procedure

> *rewrite*(*filename*)

creates the file and creates a buffer variable *filename*∧, which points at the next vacant position in the output file. The procedure

> *put*(*filename*)   or just *put* for the file *output*

moves *filename*∧ to the next position in the output file. Notice that it does not actually put anything in the buffer! You can do this yourself through the pointer, or use:

> *write*(*filename,item*)

which is the same as

> ```
> begin filename∧:=item; put(filename) end
> ```

We already know the meaning of *write* with a longer list of items, and of *writeln* with a list of items. The procedure *writeln*, which is available only on text files, is not explicitly defined in terms of *put*. Its final act when used is to *write* the sequence of characters used to end a line on your computer, and then point the buffer variable at the beginning of a new, empty line.

7 Problems

Problem 18.1 Using pointers combined with record types and files, many different tasks can be undertaken in data processing. You could, for example, spend six months writing your own editor. However let us try something more directly personal and less ambitious. Create a compact disc indexing system in which there is a master disc index, along with cross-referenced indices of composers, works and artists. Design and implement a program for maintaining the index. Of particular importance is the way in which new recordings are added, with the the cross-references automatically updated. Remember that many discs have several works by different composers possibly played by different artists. Then implement the program which enables you to refer to the index by disc, composer, work or artist.

Appendix
A Summary of Pascal

1 Pascal standards

Pascal has been standardized by the International Standards Organization as ISO 7185-1982 which is identical with the US standard ANSI/IEEE 770 X3.97-1983 and the British Standard BS 6192:1982. The British standard is definitive of the English text and the French standard NZ Z 65-300 defines the French text. It is incorrect to refer to any other version as 'standard' Pascal.

The ISO standard defines the syntax (grammar) and semantics (meaning) of Pascal. There are aspects of both which are implementation dependent, and the means of editing, compiling, loading and running a Pascal program are also implementation dependent. The standard is virtually incomprehensible to real people, and this is why books about Pascal are necessary.

2 Pascal programs (see also Chapter 10)

A Pascal program is a *heading* followed by a *block*. The *heading* is the compulsory **program** statement, and the *block* consists of optional *declarations* followed by an *action*.

> **program** *name options*;   {compulsory heading}
> *declarations*;
> *action*.   {ends with a full stop}

The optional *declarations* must define every identifier used by the *action*. The *declarations* can be any of the following, which must be given in order separated by semicolons:

> *declarations*   **label**;
> **const**;
> **type**;
> **var**;
> **procedures** or **functions**;

The **procedure** and **function** declarations are themselves *headings* which contain their own *block*. Refer to Chapter 10 for a discussion of the block structure and the scope of identifiers in Pascal.

The *action* consists of one compound statement:

> **begin** *statement*; *statement* . . . **end**.

The full stop or period shown occurs only at the end of a Pascal program.

3 Semicolons (see also Chapter 10)

Semicolons are used to separate the statements in any statement sequence, but not to terminate it. A null statement may exist which has the effect of allowing extra semicolons wherever a statement sequence is allowed—in the **begin** . . . **end** structure and the **repeat** . . . **until** structure. Therefore a semicolon is optional before **end** or **until**. A semicolon is forbidden before **else**.

4 Comments (see also Chapter 2)

Comments are initiated by the symbol { or the alternative (*, as long as it does not occur within a character string. Once initiated, all characters are part of a comment until it is terminated by } or *). Note that you can lose all or part of your program by leaving out the termination of a comment.

5 Symbols

Except in character data or strings, upper and lower case versions of the same alphabetic letter in Pascal have the same meaning. Therefore **BEGIN** is the same keyword as **begin** or any corresponding mixture of upper and lower case letters.

Pascal requires the following symbols:

> the alphabet, upper or lower case or both
> the digits 0−9
> special symbols:
> > $+ - * / = < >$
> > . , : ; ( )
> > $<= >= :=$ .. {usually pairs of symbols}
> these have alternatives:
> > { or (* } or *)
> > [or (.] or .)
> > ↑ or ∧ or @

6 Identifiers (see also Chapter 6)

An identifier in Pascal is a series of letters and digits, beginning with a letter, which in principle can have any length and all characters should be significant. Identifiers are used to name a type, constant, variable, field of a record, function, procedure, file or directive.

These are keywords or 'word-symbols' in Pascal which cannot be used as identifiers.

and	do	function	nil	program	type
array	downto	goto	not	record	until
begin	else	if	of	repeat	var
case	end	in	or	set	while
const	file	label	packed	then	with
div	for	mod	procedure	to	

A number of Pascal identifiers are predefined. They can be taken over by a declaration but then lose their predefined meaning within the scope of that declaration. These are the predefined identifiers:

types	*boolean char integer real*
constants	*false maxint true nil*
variables	*input*∧ *output*∧
functions	*abs arctan chr cos eof eoln exp ln odd ord*
	pred round sin sqr sqrt succ trunc
procedures	*get reset rewrite put* (Chapter 16)
	read readln write writeln (Chapter2)
	dispose new (Chapter 16)
	pack unpack (Chapter13)
files	*input output* (Chapter 16)
directives	*external forward* (Chapter 9)

7 The declarations

Declarations give a meaning to identifiers or labels within the scope of the declaration, which is from the point that the identifier is used to the end of the block that these declarations are in, except for record field identifiers which apply only to accesses to that record. An identifier or label can be redefined within an enclosed block (a procedure or function). It can also be suspended as an identifier within the scope of a **with** statement if the accessed record activates a name as a field identifier. It is not a very good idea to allow identifiers to change their meaning in either of these ways. (See Sermon on the Scope, Chapter 10).

The **label** declaration   (Chapter 7)

> **label** *number, number, number* . . . ;

declares labels to be used as the targets of **goto** statements. The *number*s look like integers in the range 0 to 9999 but they are labels, not integers. Every label declared must occur in the action part of the block.

The **const** declaration   (Chapter 6 and elsewhere)

> **const** *name* = *constant*;
> *name* = *constant*;
> ⋮

gives *name*s to *constant*s of the basic types real, integer, boolean, char or character strings. The type of the *name* is implied by the constant.

The **type** declaration   (Chapter 15)

> **type** *name*=*type spec*;
> *name*=*type spec*;
> ⋮   ⋮

gives a *name* (only one) to a data type constructed according to the *type spec.* See later sections for the composition of simple or particular structured types.

The **var** declaration   (Chapter 6 and elsewhere)

> **var** *name, name, name . . . :type spec*;
> *name, name, name . . . :type spec*;
> :   :

identifies the *name* and *type* of variables. The *type spec* might be the name of a specific type or a *type specification.* There are advantages in naming a type with **type** before declaring the variables with **var**—such variables can be assigned and passed as parameters to procedures or functions.

The **function** and **procedure** declarations and their parameters are dealt with separately in Sections 20 to 24 of this Appendix.

8 Simple types

The simple types include the basic types of Pascal, subranges of the basic types and enumerated types that can be created by a **type** declaration.

The basic types of Pascal are:

> *real* (Chapter 3), which is some range of numbers with some number of decimal places of precision. A real constant either contains a decimal point, or is written in scientific notation *number* e *sign integer.*

> Examples: 3.14   6.32e+23

> The real type is different from the other simple types in that it is not ordered. An integer value can always be substituted when a real number is called for.

> *integer* (Chapter 4) represents the whole numbers over at least the range −*maxint* to *maxint.* An integer constant is a number with no decimal point, for example 6491 is an integer.

> *boolean* (Chapter 5) with constant values *false* or *true.* Ord(*false*) is 0, ord(*true*) is 1.

> *char* (Chapter 13) which includes the symbols known to Pascal and possibly some others. See Chapter 13 for a discussion of the characters available and their ordering. The ASCII code for characters is listed in Section 25 of this Appendix. A character constant is any available symbol written between single quotes, e.g. 'b'. A string constant contains several such symbols, e.g. 'abcd'. The quote itself can be included by giving it in pairs, e.g. 'isn''t' is the character constant which spells the word *isn't.*

You can create a subrange of these types except real in a **type** declaration or make a subrange variable in a **var** declaration (Chapter 15).

You can create a simple type of your own, called an enumerated type (Chapter 15).

9 Declaring simple types

A type identifier is declared by a **type** declaration:

type *type name*=*type spec*;

Type spec can be the name of a type, but that is useless because it merely gives an existing type another name.

To create an enumerated type, *type spec* is a list of new identifiers in the desired order contained in brackets, which are all possible constants of that type (Chapter 15).

```
type rainbow=(red,orange,yellow,green,blue,violet);
```

To create a subrange type, *type spec* identifies a range of values of an ordered basic type or an enumerated type defined previously(Chapter 15). For example,

```
byte=-128..127;
warm=red..green;
```

It is always possible to create a variable by spelling out its *type spec* in a **var** declaration, but it then cannot be assigned or passed as a procedure or function parameter unless the *type spec* was a *type name* only. (The conformant array parameter is an exception.)

10 Using simple types

All the simple types except real are ordered, so as constants can be used for selecting in **case** structures, as variables declared in the same block can be used as the index of a **for** loop, and as values can be used as indices in subscripting arrays. For any ordered type the counting functions *ord*, *succ* and *pred* will work.

You can assign items of simple type as long as the *value* is of the same basic type as the *variable*, and lies in the permitted range of the *variable*. An integer *value* may be assigned to a real *variable* (it is first converted to real).

variable:=*value*;

You can always compare any items of the same simple type, and also items which are subranges of the same basic type whether or not their ranges overlap. An integer may be compared to a real:

value   *relational operator*   *value*

11 Expressions

Real or integer values can be used in arithmetic expressions (Chapters 3 and 7).

value   *operator*   *value*

Between real or integer values the following operations can be used:

> \+   addition
> \-   subtraction
> *   multiplication
> /   real division

The result of these operations is real if either operand was real, otherwise integer. A numerical expression with a real in it anywhere will turn out real.

The following operations can be used between integers only, and produce an integer result:

> **div**   truncated division
> **mod**   remainder

The relational operations (Chapter 5) can be done between any values of the same simple type, recalling that an integer can always be substituted for a real, or between strings of the same length:

> =   equal
> <>   not equal
> <   less than
> >   greater than
> <=   less than or equal (different meaning for sets; see Chapter 15)
> >=   greater than or equal (different meaning for sets; see Chapter 15)
> **in**   (only used with sets; see Chapter 15)

The result of a relational expression is always boolean.

The following operations can be done between boolean values only:

> **and**
> **or**

These operations are monadic, taking one operand only:

> **not**   *boolean value*
> \+   *real or integer value*
> \-   *real or integer value*

The priority of all operations is:

> ( )   (expressions in brackets)
> **not**
> *** / div mod and**   (operators like multiplication)
> **+ − or**   (operators like addition or signs)
> relational operators

12 Structured types

Structured types are collections of items of simple type in either **packed** or unpacked form. Packing is intended where possible to make a structure more compact in storage, but if it does, it will also probably make it slower to access. Procedures are provided for packing and unpacking (Chapter 15).

The **array** type collects items of one type so that type can be accessed by subscripts (Chapters 12 and 14).

The **set** type includes or excludes objects of one ordered type from a classification (Chapter 15).

The **record** type assembles items of varying type into a structure (Chapter 16).

The **file** type is your window onto an external device for data of any type except another file (Chapter 17).

A value of structured type can be assigned to a variable as long as the same **type** identifier is used to describe them (it is not sufficient for the types to be specified similarly in the **var** declaration).

> *variable*: = *value*

As there are no expressions using structured types other than sets, in practice the *value* will always be the name of another variable except with sets.

An item of structured type can be passed to a procedure or function only if it uses the same type identifier as the corresponding formal parameter (it is not sufficient for the types to be specified similarly). An item from within a packed structure cannot be used as a **var** parameter, except that an item of type char from a string can be used with the *read* or *readln* procedures.

13 Arrays and subscripts (Chapters 12, 14)

An array type which collects values of any one type can be formed in the **type** or **var** declaration by giving the *type specification*:

> **array**[*min1* . . *max1,min2* . . *max2* . . .] **of** *type spec*

or, if packed, substitute **packed array** for **array**.

Min1 and *max1* are the smallest and largest values of the first index and are constants of the same simple ordered type which will be used for that index, and so on for as many subscripts as are used.

A value from an array variable is accessed using an index of the correct type lying in the declared range:

> *arrayname*[*index*]

Multidimensional arrays use several indices:

>   *name*[*index1,index2* . . .]

Alternatively, a multidimensional array could be declared as an array of arrays:

>   **array**[*min1 . . max1*] **of array**[*min2 . . max2*] **of** *type spec*

in which case it would be indexed by

>   *name*[*index1*][*index2*] . . .

14 Strings (Chapter 13)

A string variable of a particular length is a **packed array** [1 . . *length*] **of** *char*, and is permitted some privileges in Pascal not allowed to other structured types.

Strings of the same *length* (not necessarily using the same identifiers) can be assigned:

>   *string variable*: = *string value*   {*string value* is a variable or constant}

Strings of the same *length* can be compared:

>   *string value*   *relational operator*   *string value*

and a single character from within a string can be defined by the *read* or *readln* statements, for example if *thing* is a string type and *i* is an integer in the index range of *thing*:

>   *read*(*thing*[*i*])

Note that an **array of** *char* which is not **packed** is not a string.

A string constant is a sequence of symbols enclosed by single quotation marks unless these are part of a comment. Quotes may be included in strings by doubling up, for example in this string constant of length 17:

>   'Isn''t this clear?'

15 Sets (Chapter 15)

A **set** is a structure which includes or excludes items from some range of an ordered type. It is declared in either a **var** or **type** declaration using the *type spec*:

>   **set of** *ordered type spec*

Items can be assigned to a set variable from a range expression:

>   *variable*: = [*min . . max*]

Operations between set variables or range expressions form new set values:

+	union	(combine the values)
*	intersection	(only the common values)
−	difference	(remove the common values)

The relational operators have special meaning when used between set values:

set value = set value
>   *true* if the sets contain exactly the same values, *false* otherwise

set value <> set value
>   *true* if the sets do not contain exactly the same values, *false* otherwise

set a <= set b
>   *true* if *set a* is contained in *set b*

set a >= set b
>   *true* if *set b* is contained in *set a*

value **in** *set value*
>   *true* if the value of the base type is contained in the set

16 Records (Chapter 16)

The record type, used as a *type spec* in either the **var** or **type** declaration, collects values of different type together into one structure.

>   **record**
>   *field, field, . . . field: type spec;*
>   *field, field, . . . field: type spec;*
>   :
>   *at most one variant part*
>   **end**;

Each *field* is a unique identifier in the particular **record** delaration,but could be the same as some item in another declaration. The variant part if present must be the last one:

>   **case** *ordered type name* **of**
>   *constant, constant* . . . : (*field definitions*);
>   *constant,* . . .
>   :

or with a *tag field*:

>   **case** *tag name: ordered type name* **of**
>   :

The *tag name* if it is used restricts access to the variant selected by the field called *tag name*. If it is not used, all the variants are available at once. The lists of *constants* must cover all the possible values of the *ordered type* used to select. An empty variant

>   *constant, constant* . . . : ();

can be used to collect the values of the *ordered type* that are not wanted.

An item from within a record variable is referred to using the record variable's name and the *field name*:

> *record name . field name*

If the field is itself a record, multiple constructions can occur:

> *record . field name . field name . field name* . . .

The **with** statement in the action part of a Pascal program opens a particular records so that their fields can be referred to directly by their *field names*:

> **with** *record name, record name* . . . **do** *statement*

This can have the effect of redefining identifiers within the **with** structure.

17 Files, input and output (Chapter 17)

It may be necessary to name the files used by a Pascal program in the **program** declaration. The exact form of the **program** declaration is implementation dependent.

The normal input file (probably your keyboard) is called *input*. The normal output file (probably your screen) is called *output*. *Input* and *output* are predefined.

Other files can be used if they are declared as variables whose type is specified in a **type** or **var** declaration as

> **file of** *type spec*

The *type spec* may not itself contain a type which includes a file.

The special type *text* is a **file of** *char*, and allows all the symbols known to your Pascal plus an end of line indicator. *Input* and *output* are *text*.

A file may be opened for input by the procedure *reset*:

> *reset(file variable name)*

A file may be opened for output by the procedure *rewrite*:

> *rewrite(file variable name)*

Both *reset* and *rewrite* create a file buffer variable *file variable name*∧ of the type of the file. The buffer variable contains the next input value for an input file, and the next output value is put into this buffer for an output file. The procedures *reset(input)* and *rewrite(output)* are done for you before the action part of your Pascal program commences.

(i)   Reading

The procedure *read(filename, variable, variable . . .*) obtains information sequentially from the file *filename* which must be of the correct type. For the file *input* the *filename* can be omitted.

A text file can provide only reals, integers or single characters.

The procedure *readln* is avaiable only for text files. It moves to a new line of input after the final *variable* has been read.

The boolean function *eof(filename)*, or just *eof* for the input file, is normally *false*, but becomes *true* when there is no more information in an input file.

The boolean function *eoln(filename)*, or just *eoln* for the input file, is normally *false* but becomes *true* when there are no more characters on a line for a file of text. It becomes *false* again when the end of line itself is read, which is passed back as a space. Then the next character read is the beginning of a new line. Many Pascal implementations do not follow this for interactive files.

(ii)   Writing

Values of the correct type are passed to a file by the *write* procedure:

$$\text{write(}\textit{filename, value, value, . . .}\text{)}$$

For the file *output* the *filename* may be omitted.

For text files, the values written can be reals, integers, booleans and characters or character strings. The procedure *writeln* for text files moves to a new line after the information has been written.

For text files, any item can be written with a *width* specification which must be an integer expression giving a value > 0:

$$\textit{value: width}$$

The real type is written in scientific notation (*value* e *exponent*) unless both *width* and *decimalplaces* specifications are given:

$$\textit{value: width: decimalplaces}$$

Both *read* and *write* are defined in terms of buffer procedures *put* and *get*. See Chapter 18.

18   Pointers

Variables declared by the **var** declaration and referred to by their names are static variables, created when a program, procedure or function is activated and present throughout any particular activation. Pascal also provides for dynamic variables which can be created and disposed of at any time and in any numbers (in principle). These do not have their own names, but are pointed at by pointer variables. To get a structure started, a **pointer** *type spec* is used in either a **type** or **var** declaration:

$\wedge$*type name*

As the only exception to the 'define before use' rule, the *type name* may be defined later in the same **type** declaration. A pointer variable is then used in creating a dynamic variable of the desired type when the program activates the procedure *new*:

new(*pointer variable name*)

Subsequently, the dynamic variable is referred to using the pointer as

pointer variable name$\wedge$

The *dispose* procedure discards the dynamic variable and makes the space it occupies available again:

dispose(*pointer variable name*)

A particular variant of a variant record is created by giving constant values for the *tag* fields:

new(*pointer variable name, tag, tag, tag, . . .*)

which then has to be discarded by giving the same constants

dispose(*pointer variable name, tag, tag, tag, . . .*)

19 Statements

The following is a list of the statements which might occur in the action part of a Pascal program.

The compound statement

begin *statement*; *statement*; . . . *statement* **end**

The activation of a procedure

procedure name(*parameters*)   (Chapter 9)

The assignment of a value

variable name:=*value*

Structured statements (Chapters 6, 7)

if *boolean value* **then** *true statement*

If the *boolean value* is *true* the *true statement* is taken, otherwise the program continues beyond the **if** structure.

if *boolean value* **then** *true statement* **else** *false statement*

> If the *boolean value* is *true* the *true statement* is taken, otherwise the *false statement* is taken. In either case, the program then continues beyond the **if** structure.

while *boolean value* **do** *statement*

> If the *boolean value* is *true* the *statement* is taken, and then the **while** is repeated. Otherwise the program continues beyond the **while** structure. A **while** loop is an iteration in which the stopping condition is checked at the beginning.

repeat *statement*; *statement* . . . ; *statement* **until** *boolean value*

> All the *statement*s are taken. Then if the *boolean value* is *false*, they are repeated again. Otherwise the program continues beyond the **repeat** structure. A **repeat** . . . **until** loop is an iteration in which the stopping condition is checked at the end. The *statement*s in the loop are executed at least once.

for *local index*:=*low* **to** *high* **do** *statement*

> If *high*>=*low*, the statement is repeated with the *local index* taking all the values in increasing order from *low* to *high*. Otherwise the program continues beyond the **for** structure. *Local index* is a variable of an ordered type which is local to the function or procedure the **for** appears in, or global if **for** is in a main program. *Low* and *high* are values in the permitted range of the *index*.

for *local index*:=*high* **downto** *low* **do** *statement*

> If *high*>=*low*, the *statement* is repeated with the *local index* taking all the values in decreasing order from *high* to *low*. Otherwise the program continues beyond the **for** structure.

> In either version of **for**, the value of the *local index* may not be threatened in any way; by assignment, by the *read* or *readln* procedures or by being passed as a **var** parameter to a procedure or function within the **for** structure.

> A **for** structure is a loop which counts as it iterates, and the stopping condition is checked at the beginning of each iteration. As with **while** the iteration may not be taken at all, for example in:

> ```
> for ch:='z' to 'a' do writeln('Not written')
> ```

case *ordered value* **of**
  constant, constant . . . : *statement*;
  :
  constant, constant . . . : *statement*
end

> One *statement* from the structure is selected according to the value of *ordered value* where the **case** statement is taken. This value must occur in one of the list of

constants—it is an error if an unlisted *ordered value* occurs. The non-standard extension before **end**:

> **otherwise**:*statement*

is widely available.

with *record name, record name* . . . **do** *statement*;   (Chapter 16)

> In the *statement*, the fields of the named records can be referred to by their field names only. This can have the effect of redefining names within the **with** structure.

A most unpopular statement:

goto *label*

> The program next takes the statement with the *label* on it within the scope of the nearest **label** declaration which defines the *label*.

20 Functions

A function returns a result of a particular simple or pointer type and is used as part of an expression:

> *name*(*parameters*)

Functions are not available for structured types in ISO Pascal.

The built-in functions of Pascal use only value parameters.

The arithmetic functions (Chapters 3, 4) accept real or integer parameters, and return a result which is real, except that *abs* and *sqr* return a real result which is the same type as the parameter.

abs(*value*)	Absolute value of *value*.
sqr(*value*)	The square of *value*. (May not exist in computer's range.)
sin(*value*)	The sine of *value*; *value* is in radians.
cos(*value*)	The cosine of *value*; *value* is in radians.
exp(*value*)	e^{value}; e is 2.71828 . . . the base of natural logarithms.
ln(*value*)	Logarithm of *value* to base e; *value* > 0.
sqrt(*value*)	Square root of *value*; *value* >= 0.
arctan(*value*)	The angle between $-\pi/2$ and $\pi/2$, whose tangent is *value*.

The transfer functions change the type of a value from real to integer (Chapter 4).

trunc(*value*)   removal of fractional part of *value*.
          trunc(3.6) gives 3   *trunc*(−3.6) gives −3

round(*value*)   rounding of *value*

round(3.4) gives 3	*round*(3.6) gives 4
round(−3.4) gives −3	*round*(−3.6) gives −4

Counting or ordered functions. The parameter must be of ordered type.

ord(*value*)
>   The integer which is the order of *value* in the range of its type (Chapter 4).

chr(*value*)
>   The *char* result whose order is the integer *value*. The character code varies between computers but ASCII is common (see Section 25 of this Appendix). For any character set, if *symbol* is of type *char*,

$$chr(ord('symbol')) = 'symbol'$$

(Chapter 13).

succ(*value*)
>   The next value in the same type as *value* (Chapters 4, 15).

pred(*value*)
>   The previous value in the same type as *value* (Chapters 4, 15).

Boolean functions provide a *true* or *false* result:

odd(*value*)
>   *True* if the integer value is a multiple of 2, otherwise *false* (Chapters 4, 5).

eof(*filename*)   or   *eof* for the file *input*
>   *True* if there is no more information on the input file *filename*, otherwise *false* (Chapters 5, 13).

eoln(*filename*)   or   *eoln* for the file *input*
>   *True* if on the *text* file *filename* the next character is the end of line. Difficult to implement on interactive files if not impossible (Chapters 5, 13, 17).

A user-defined function forms its own block in a Pascal program, and may contain **procedure** and **function** definitions within it (Chapter 11).

>   **function** *name*(*parameters*):*simple or pointer type name*;
>   *declarations*;
>   *action*;

A function's block is activated whenever it is referred to in a block which contains it (including itself). When the function's action is completed, all the local values of variables defined by it are lost. The function can return results through **var** parameters but normally does so through the assignment of a value of the correct type to the function name within the action part of the function. This must happen.

The formation of parameters is summarized in Sections 22−24 of this Appendix.

21 Procedures

Procedures are like functions, except that they do not have a type and are activated by a separate statement (Chapter 9).

> *procedurename(parameters)*

Normally a procedure operates using its parameters.

A number of procedures are required in Pascal. Refer to the main text for detailed descriptions of those listed here, which are the standard ones:

File handling

write, writeln, read, readln	(most chapters but particularly 17)
reset, rewrite	(Chapter 17)
get, put	(Chapter 18)
page	(Chapter 17)

Dynamic variable allocation

new, dispose	(Chapter 18)

Packing and unpacking

pack, unpack	(Chapter 15)

A user-defined procedure forms its own block in a Pascal program, and may contain **procedure** and **function** definitions within it (Chapter 9).

> **procedure** *name(parameters)*;
>   *declarations*;
>   *action*;

A procedure is activated by a statement which refers to it in a block which contains it (including itself). When the procedure completes its *action*, all the local values defined by it are lost. It can return results through **var** parameters. The formation of parameters is discussed in the next sections.

22 Parameters (Chapter 9)

Parameters are an important mechanism for passing information to procedures and functions.

In the definition of the procedure or function, value and **var** parameters are distinguished. The parameters in these definitions are called formal parameters.

> *parameter list; parameter list; . . .*

where each parameter list could be either a list of value parameters:

> *name, name, name . . . : type name*

or a list of **var** or variable parameters:

> **var** *name*, *name* . . . : *type name*

A parameter can also be a procedure or function parameter, or a conformant array scheme summarized later.

For either value or **var** parameters, the *name*s define identifiers that can be treated as if they were local variables throughout the action part of the procedure.

When a program at a particular point wishes to activate a procedure or function, it does so by giving the name of it and a list of actual parameters which exactly match the types of the formal parameters in the **function** or **procedure** heading. A value parameter can be matched to any value of the correct type. A **var** parameter can only be matched to the name of a variable, possibly indexed if it is an array, which identifies a variable of the correct type.

For simple variables the only restriction is that a **for** index cannot be threatened by passing its name to a procedure which uses it as a **var** parameter.

With structured types there are other restrictions. It is often inefficient to pass a structured item as a value parameter because a copy is made of it each time, which consumes time and space. Therefore structured types should be passed as a **var** parameter. With structured types, the actual structured parameter must have the same *type name* used in its **var** declaration as in the list of formal parameters. It is not sufficient for them to be formed from the same basic types or to have similar type specifications.

A packed item from within a structured type cannot be passed as a **var** parameter either. An exception is made for *char* items forming part of a string, which can be obtained from *read* or *readln*.

A tag variable from a variant record structure may not be passed as a **var** parameter.

23 Function or procedure parameters

A complete **function** or **procedure** declaration can be put as a formal parameter. When the actual parameter is passed, it must be the name of a procedure or function which is known to both the activating statement and the procedure being called. This means that both must be declared in the same block. Examples are given in Chapters 9 and 11.

24   Conformant array parameters

A conformant array parameter is written in the **procedure** or **function** heading as:

> *name*: **array**[*min1* . . *max1*: *type spec*; *min2* . . *max2*: *type spec* . . .]
> **of** *type spec*

or

> **var** *name*: **array**[*min1* . . *max1*: *type spec*; *min2* . . *max2*: *type spec* . . .]
> **of** *type spec*

Here not only is *name* available as a variable throughout the procedure, but so are the values *min1*, *max1*, and so on (but they are not available for assignment). The *type spec* can be either a further conformant array or a *type name*.

In the activation, the name of an array defined as having the correct number and type of indices and formed from the same type must be used. The procedure then picks up the index bounds automatically. A value conformant array parameter cannot be passed to a further procedure as a **var** parameter. It is best to use **var** parameters anyway. Only the last array description in a conformant array scheme can be **packed**. Examples of conformant array parameters are given in Chapters 12, 13 and 14.

25 The ASCII code

Listed here is the character value and order of all the printable symbols in the ASCII code. The non-printing symbols CR (carriage return) and LF (linefeed) are also often of interest. However there is a wide variation between computer software and peripherals about whether a sender follows a CR with an explicit LF, or whether the receiver is supposed to assume one.

ord('symbol')	symbol	ord('symbol')	symbol	ord('symbol')	symbol
10	LF	63	?	95	—
13	CR	64	@	96	`
32	space	65	A	97	a
33	!	66	B	98	b
34	"	67	C	99	c
35	#	68	D	100	d
36	$	69	E	101	e
37	%	70	F	102	f
38	&	71	G	103	g
39	'	72	H	104	h
40	(	73	I	105	i
41	)	74	J	106	j
42	*	75	K	107	k
43	+	76	L	108	l
44	,	77	M	109	m
45	−	78	N	110	n
46	.	79	O	111	o
47	/	80	P	112	p
48	0	81	Q	113	q
49	1	82	R	114	r
50	2	83	S	115	s
51	3	84	T	116	t
52	4	85	U	117	u
53	5	86	V	118	v
54	6	87	W	119	w
55	7	88	X	120	x
56	8	89	Y	121	y
57	9	90	Z	122	z
58	:	91	[	123	{
59	;	92	\	124	|
60	<	93	]	125	}
61	=	94	∧	126	~
62	>				

Index